T0316618

Women Musicians of Zimbabwe Diary
by
Joyce Jenje Makwenda

Chengetayi Razemba performing in France

Joyce Jenje Makwenda
P.O. Box M163, Mabelreign
Harare, Zimbabwe
joycejenje@gmail.com

ISBN: 978 0 7974 5485 9

Year Planner

January

February

March

April

May

June

Year Planner

July	August

September	October

November	December

Personal Details

Name   :...

....

Address   :...

....

....

Home Telephone Number   :...

Fax   :...

Work Telephone Number   :...

Fax   :...

Identity Number   :...

Passport Number   :...

Driving License No.   :...

Car Registration Number   :...

Insurance Policy Number   :...

Bank Account Number   :...

Medical Doctor   :...

Dentist   :...

Holistic Practitioner   :...

Pharmacy   :...

Allergies   :...

Blood Group   :...

Medical Aid No   :...

Lawyer   :...

with the more powerful. In some instances a daughter-in-law would reverse the roles by addressing her mother-in-law as her daughter-in-law.

This swapping of places made it easier for the younger woman to say what she wanted to say to her mother-in-law. (The naming of children by a daughter-in-law was also used as a communication tool, to register her concern to her in-laws, names like Sarudzayi (Discriminate), Tambudzayi (You make me suffer), Nyarai (Be ashamed), Muchaneta (You will get tired), Godknows, Norest, Nodivorce, Last etc.)

Today women cannot challenge their husbands and remind them of their duties because of the so-called civilisation. It questions what we mean by civilisation and the so-called primitive cultures which, allowed women a voice. 'Civilised cultures' thrive on sweeping things under the carpet by wanting to paint a good picture to make people think things are okay whilst so-called primitive cultures thrived on recognising the basics of life.

WOMEN CONTINUE TO USE MUSIC AS A COMMUNICATION TOOL AND CELEBRATE YOUR WOMANHOOD!

Lina Mattaka

A refined soprano and tap-dancer, Lina Mattaka set jazz aflame in the African townships, defying a tradition which confined women to church choirs. She also taught young girls tap dancing.

While singing for her church in Bulawayo in the 1930s, her career blossomed when her Church Choir toured Simonstown in South Africa. On her return she joined the Bantu Glee Singers, led by a Mr. Sipambaniso. She was later nicknamed Queen of Soprano. Lina married Kenneth Mattaka in 1944, who performed with the Bantu Actors she also joined the Bantu Actors. She later sang with her family; children Bertha and Eddison, and Kenneth, making the Mattaka Family Group.

Lina Mattaka was also featured in a radio programme the Mattaka Family which was produced by Ephraim Chamba in 1959, for the Federal Broadcasting Corporation (FBC). She also took part in the film: "Mattaka Buys a Bicycle," with her husband Kenneth Mattaka and her daughter Bertha, and appeared in a 15-20 minute film, with brother Eddison on piano. In 1998 she featured in a documentary - The Bantu Actors/Mattaka Family (A Family Musical Group which goes back to the 50's).

> *Lina Mattaka's singing career is perhaps the longest on record. She very well deserves being termed the greatest of the women pioneers. For it is Lina in those stale curtain-laced years, the late thirties who alone championed the women's cause. In the larger cities, there were times, so she tells me, when a woman was not so readily welcome on stage. But Lina and jazz came rolling was among the first few women who joined to set the Ball of Jazz Rolling the Jazz-O-Africa Townships rolling'(4, February 1958 – Socialite –The African Daily News).*

At the inaugural Harare Jazz Festival Lifetime Achievement Award Lina Mattaka was honoured for her contribution and championing early township music/jazz.

Evelyn Juba

Evelyn Juba came on the music scene immediately after Lina Mattala and in the 1930s they were the only notable women in the popular music scene. She sang with her husband Simon Juba, and her brother Remmington Mazabane, which electrified Bulawayo audiences in the 1930s. Evelyn sang makwaya (choir), swing and jazz.

"There was no entertainment in the townships, so we had to create entertainment ourselves," Evelyn said.

She defied traditional gender roles that confined women to child rearing and cooking, and took the showbiz by storm, performing all over the country and neighbouring Botswana (then Bechuanaland), where some Bamangwato fans journeyed for several days on foot or horseback to Serowe to hear her [Evelyn] sing.

> "Concert goers of the early 1936 would focus on the name; Evelyn Juba. Eve, as fans in showbiz knew her, held sway in musical showbiz until 1952, long after the advent of the old jazz era. She soon retired from active stage work to give more attention to her growing family, having been active for more than 16 years. Such an achievement is her singular honour and memorable contribution. Evelyn Juba made her debut in Bulawayo during 1936, at the newly built Stanley Hall with the Merry Makers." (8 March 1958- Socialite –African Daily News).

In 1992 together with her husband she was featured in a film documentary – Zimbabwe Township Music.

Rennie Jones Nyamundanda

ifteen years ago, as Miss Rennie Jones, the bright young singer and star of the stage, Mrs. Nyamundanda made a terrific debut in Salisbury's Harare African Township. That was her first appearance on the stage. She was singing with a young group which had just been started by leader and singer Fancy Mpahlo. It is Fancy and Rennie who made that wonderful two-some. Together they tapped, danced and crooned the music of the African setting. They mixed ancient with old, and sang in the mines, schools as well as in towns. Whenever they sang they were hailed by packed houses. She was thus the first woman to sing with the Follies.

During those two eventful years she sang with the Follies she won for herself the title of Harare's most popular female stage artist. But ….., how short lived her glory was!

…so much did she do during those two crowning years that now, many years after she is gone posterity still remembers her as one of the few bold women who paved the way for the African woman on stage. But how far those days seem to be from the present Jazz Era?

Yes they were all heralding the coming of JAZZ-O-AFRICAN TOWNSHIPS." (8 February 1958)

Dorothy Masuka

Born in Bulawayo in 1935, she moved to Johannesburg as a small girl and began her professional career there in 1951. Dorothy Masuka has been in the music scene for more than 60 years. Popularly and affectionately known as Dotty, Dorothy Masuka composed and recorded more than any artist in the 1950's. A prolific composer, some of her popular songs were; Hamba noNsokolo, Imali yami iphelele eshabhini, UNolitshwa and UMalani ulomuthetho onzima, these songs represent but a small portion of the extensive Masuka catalogue.

She introduced new lyrics, new dressing, and new stage work. Dorothy sang about shabeens, about fashion, about politics. Her lyrics reflected what was happening in the society in the 1950s. She began singing as a jazz singer in Sophiatown, South Africa, where she sometimes staged shows with Dolly Rathebe, Miriam Makeba and maestro Kippie Moeketsi. Her popular tune "Hamba Nontsokolo", is an all-time household hit. In Zimbabwe she also performed with major musical groups of the 50's, including the Gay Gaeties, The De Black Evening Follies, The City Quads. Dorothy was a big stage and recording star in South Africa in the 1950s but eventually had to leave the country because of her outspoken political views. She spent the 1960s and 70s in Kenya and Zambia, where she continued to record, before returning to live in Zimbabwe after independence. In the early 1990s, Dorothy took up residence in Johannesburg and frequently tours the continent and internationally. Masuka, was once married to Dusty King {Freddie Gotora}, a one-time Zimbabwean star footballer of the 50s. Dorothy has been in the music industry for 60 years making her the musician who stayed longest in music here in Zimbabwe and one of the few in Southern Africa.In 2007 she was honoured with a degree in Sociology by the Africa Women's University (Harare) and in 2011 in March she was honoured at the inaugural Harare Jazz Festival Lifetime Achievement Award Jazz Festival for her contribution to township jazz music.

Date

Date

Date

THE GRAND OLD DAMES OF SHOWBIZ:
They dedicated their lives to championing show business

In the not-so distant past, a woman who performed popular music was considered by society to be a fallen woman, most commonly a prostitute. Despite the negative attitude, women musicians in Zimbabwe championed their liberation by becoming active in show business. They travelled the thorny highway of music setting free their enterprising African spirit.

These women suffered all forms of oppression - of gender, class and race the list goes on. They confronted cultural and social colonialism not by rejecting outside influences but by linking with the progressive elements of international music, which they subjected to the disciplines and traditions of the indigenous music. In the process, they created a new, outward-looking art form, a fusion popularly known as "Township Jazz," a mixture of American jazz (which was originally influenced by African music) and African traditional music. Township jazz was performed, especially in South Africa and Zimbabwe, in the regions where black people lived. It was culturally rich and politically relevant, and it expressed the way of life in the colonial period.

There was no entertainment in the townships and they made the township a better place to live. Some women were more prominent than others, but they all helped in shaping and paving the way for today's women. They did not only set the ball of jazz rolling in the townships, but they are pacesetters for todays popular music be it gospel, urban grooves ect.

Lina Mattaka was a township jazz innovator. Her musical career started in the late 1930s in Bulawayo, the second largest city in the country. After her marriage to the musician Kenneth Mattaka, she moved to the capital, Salisbury (called Harare since independence), and sometimes performed with their daughter, Bertha Mattaka-Msora, who started singing at the age of five. Bertha became a well known playwright, actress and educator, thereby dispelling the commonly-held viewpoint that women musicians were social misfits. Lina Mattaka groomed female musicians whom she brought into the Bantu Actors. These were Thandi Sheba, Charlotte Phiri and Renny

Jones. Her home was like a cultural center were young people were taught to sing and play instruments.

Evelyn Juba was to follow in the footsteps of Lina Mattaka, a singer from Bulawayo, electrified her audiences beginning in the late 1930s. She performed with her husband, Simon Juba, and a group called the Merry Makers. The Merry Makers included other talented women such as Agnes Zengeni, who claimed that music is like any other talent. She admonished critics and advised women that they should not be ashamed to become musicians. Another successful performer was Emma Dube(Mrs Tafi), who was nicknamed "Judy Garland", the mother of Liza Minneli. Musicians wanted to identify themselves with African-American Jazz Artists since they are the ones they were emulating.

 In the 1950s Dorothy Masuka was considered the number one jazz singer in the country and in South Africa, and she was Grammy Awards winning South African singer Miriam Makeba's idol. Masuka staged shows with Dolly Ratebe (of the film "Jim goes to Jo'burg" the first black film to be made in South Africa). Dorothy Masuku has been in the music scene for 60 years, she is the longest serving woman musicians and musician in general in Southern Africa.

Victoria Chingate, a nurse at the hospital (now called the Harare Hospital), formed an all-female singing group made up of nurses who called themselves the Gay Gaeties. When they made their debut, audiences were surprised that educated women would take up a career they had always associated with the uneducated. At the hospital, the white nurses had their own social gatherings and Christmas parties, which excluded the black nurses. When the Gay Gaeties was formed, the white nurses became attracted to the music and eventually joined the Gay Gaeties at social gatherings. This proved to be a major step forward in destroying colour-barriers at the hospital.

In the 1950s the late Sylvia Sondo formed an all-female troupe called the Yellow Blues, which included Susan Chenjerayi who became a renowned musician of the 60's-70's. One of the most celebrated musician of the 50's was Faith Dauti. The Shot Gun Boogie as she was popularly known, was one of the hottest women musicians.

Together with her brother and two cousins they formed the Milton Brothers. She also sang with the City Quads, the Golden Rhythym Crooners, the Gay Gaeties and Simanga Tutani with Chris Chabuka.

The Africa Daily News commented that "Faith Dauti was heard on the radio more often than the time check."

Renny Jones who was later known to be Mrs Nyamundanda, was the first woman to sing with the De Black Evening Follies apopular township music group from the 40's -60's. The De Black Evening Follies brought in many women in their band in the 50s.

Joyce Ndoro was one of them and she stayed with the De Black Evening Follies for a long time. She was also crowned Miss Harare while she was with the De Black Evening Follies. She was popularly known for her song Goli Goli which was taught to her by Indians at an inter-cultural show.

Other women who joined the De Black Evening Follies were Mabel Bingwa and Kristine Dube. These two were discovered at a talent show which the De Black Evening Follies held every Christmas.

Sylivia Benya who changed her name to Sondo when she married the maestro of music Sonny Sondo also started at the De Black Evening Follies. She later came up with her own group which was all-female trupe called the Yellow Blues. It is in this group that Susan Chenjerayi of the Amai Rwizi fame was groomed. Besides singing, Sylivia Sondo worked as a nurse.

Flora Dick and Margaret Pazarangu also made their mark in the music scene and they sang with a band called the Mashonaland Melodians, which was led by Albert Ndinda.

In 1954 Victoria Chingate took the country by storm when she started an all-female group called the Gay Gaeties. The Gay Gaeties made their debut at the Harare Hospital. The all-female group was composed of nurses. People were surprised that educated women could take up a career normally associated with uneducated women.

The Gay Gaeties was formed out of frustration as the white nurses had their own Christmas parties which excluded Black nurses. The formation of the Gay Gaeties was a step in destroying colour bar at the hospital as the white nurses started mixing with the black nurses.

It then became fashionable for musical groups to have a female vocalist.

The Golden Rhythym Croones sang with Rose Sedman who was from Cape Town. Sedman also sang with the Bulawayo-based group the Cool Four. Valerie Govenda who was likened to Ella Fitzgerald sang with Pat Travers and the Arcadia Rhythym Lads.

Ruth Mpisaunga and Sara Gutu sang with Jeremiah Kainga. They are known for the popular song Imi Munosara Nani Ndaenda which was composed by Jeremiah Kainga. Sara Mabokela (Mhlanga) who was also popular in the 1950s did her own version of Imi Munosara Nani Ndaenda with the Mahotella Queens in the 60s and it became very popular.

Tabeth Kapuya started singing with Victoria Chingate and later became a celebrity in her own right. Martha Banda also crooned with the City Quads and re-recorded Ndafuna-funa with with the group.

The early women musicians told of how smart they used to look. Chemicals for African hair had not been introduced in the country. They would stretch their hair with a heated stone to make it easier to comb.

They would put on stiff dresses over mosquito net petticoats, figure hugging bottom dresses and 'bougarel' trousers and high heeled shoes.

'We used to look good because we took time to groom ourselves for our shows,' said Tabeth Kapuya. Tabeth had once teamed up with Simangaliso Tutani and had composed a song Uri Mudiwa Wangu Iwe Simanga (You are my love, Simanga).Simangaliso Tutani was one of the most renowened musician of the 50's.

The wonderful township jazz era came to an end in 1960s, soon after the federation was terminated and racial separation was more stringently enforced. Laws were enacted that prohibited black musicians from singing before more than one person at a time. Musical groups disbanded and musicians such as Dorothy Masuka left the country, not returning to Zimbabwe until attained its independence.

The early women musicians will go down in history as paving the way for those who later followed in their footsteps. They are the THE GRAND OLD DAMES OF SHOWBIZ – WE CELEBRATE THEM!

Date

WOMEN MUSICIANS OF ZIMBABWE

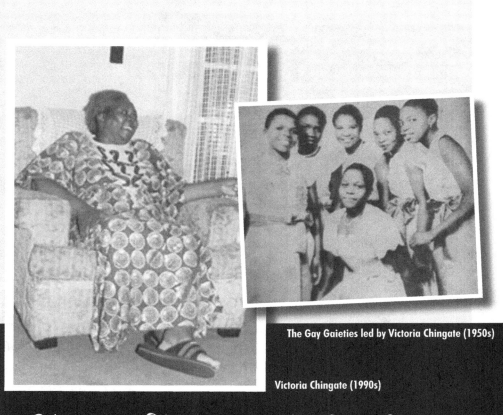

The Gay Gaieties led by Victoria Chingate (1950s)

Victoria Chingate (1990s)

Victoria Chingate & the Gay Gaeties

Victoria formed the Gay Gaeties in 1954 as a way of creating entertainment particularly around Christmas time, as the white nurses had their own separate entertainment. The group consisted of Tetiwe Solani, Grace Mandishona, Dorcas Fry, Martha Mabhena and Rose (Mrs Samkange). She said that when the Gay Gaeties were formed it brought the two races together as the Gay Gaeties' parties became more popular because of their music. During Christmas time, the hospital authorities would give the Gay Gaeties the task of organizing a Christmas show for the hospital, which was attended by all races. This demonstrates that music crosses racial boundaries and can bring people together.

The Gay Gaeities' fan base was composed of a wide spectrum of society and amongst them political leaders who were mostly brought by Victoria's husband, Scotting Chingate, who was a politician and an MP for the Federation of Rhodesia and Nyasaland. This attracted patrons of significant status in society.

While earlier women musicians had not been viewed as a threat to the cultural expectations (they were seen as role models of a descent marriage and home), the Gay Gaeties on the other hand gained their respect because they were educated formally.

The Gay Gaieties destroyed the myth that music was for the so-called 'social misfits' including the uneducated women. Initially some people were surprised to see educated women like Victoria and the nurses taking to music, more so being an all female group. One female teacher asked Victoria why a woman would choose to perform in the public. She said, "When I came to the show I wanted to see what a woman can do in a public like this, but the music was good and I had fun."

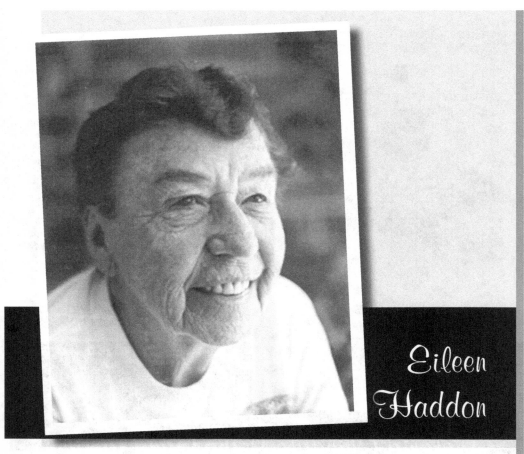

Eileen Haddon

In the 50's it was not usual for blacks and whites to mix socially. Eileen Haddon, used music as a tool to fight colour bar (racial discrimination), a journalist, and founder member of the Inter-Racial Association, decided to change the situation by organising inter-racial cultural events.

"When I organised the inter-racial music show at the Salisbury showgrounds, I thought only a few white liberals would come," said Eileen. "To my surprise, the stadium was so packed that we ran out of food. Many whites came, and what suprised them most was the township groups could sing so well." Eileen also turned one of her rooms in her house into a music hall where she brought some of the early popular musicans, like Alick Nkata and Moses Mpahlo to perform. One enthusiastic visitor, struck by the contrast with racially divided Salisbury commented, "In this house it's like I am in Brazil."

With all the efforts that a woman like Eileen had put into trying to destroy racism, unfortunately the political situation became unstable, a state of emergency was introduced, and in 1963 musicians were not allowed to sing for more than one person. This saw many musicians leaving the country going into exile in Zambia, which had achieved its independence in 1964. Eileen Haddon was also to find sanctuary in Zambia. Like other exiles, they only came back when Zimbabwe gained its independence.

When Zimbabwe gained its independence in 1980 when most of the people who were at the helm of the music came back, Eileen also returned to the country. Although Eileen was no longer active in the music scene she supported the music from the sidelines, and she has been documented in the Zimbabwe Township Music Documentary (Joyce Jenje Makwenda, 1992).

Barbara Tredgold

A unique supporting centre for entertainment and township music was Runyararo Hall, in Mbare's National section, Barbara Tredgold who was in charge of the Church, was also a keen patron of township entertainment. She also provided space for young groups like African Kid Brothers, which was a band of youngsters consisting of George Mambo, Shelton Mazowe (leader), Kenny Tabva, and Raphel Murambiwa. Female musicians included Faith Dauti and Mabel Bingwa. Sister Barbara often organized trips for the young performing artists, with one such outing during Rhodes and Founders Holiday in Zvishavane in the 50's. It still lingers as a memorable event to those who participated in it.

Barbara Tredgold was involved in the Runyararo Drama Group, the Drama Group later won a coveted prize at a contest which was organized by Barbara Tredgold, at the Anglican Cathedral.

Because of her popularity in the township, musical groups such as the City Quads helped raise money to build a crèche in the neighborhood, named after Sister Barbara. It was one of the best run crèches in the township, where nursery school teachers were also trained.

Barbara Tredgold used music and theatre to close the color bar that existed between blacks and whites particularly in the 50's.

Barbara Tredgold also went on to start women's clubs with Mai Musodzi born Musodzi Chibhaga.

Monica Marsden

Runyararo was famous for its Drama Club led by Monica Marsden. Several musicians belonged to this group, The Runyararo Drama Group; including Victoria Chingate and her Gay Gaeties, Sonny Sondo, Sam Matambo, Steven Mtunyani and Pat Travers of the Arcadia Rhythm Lads . Monica also produced a number of plays such as *"Cry The Beloved Country"*. The drama club became a sensation because of its able actors and the good quality of the productions. Victoria Chingate remembers how well they were received by the audience, which was mostly whites at the time. Demand for the drama group was overwhelming in the city center.

Drama played an important role in early township entertainment. The producer of the drama shows Marsden, endeavored to make life in the township a little more interesting. She also fought the color bar through entertainment, by organizing and staging drama shows in the City Centre. The white community soon realized that blacks could also act well in drama.
The group was later invited to perform at the Reps Theater.
She will always be remembered for the part she played in the advancement of Township entertainment.

Date

Date

Date

Ambuya Rena Chitombo

reams are a strong force in the spiritual world as they are seen as the ways ancestors communicate with the living. According to Veit Erlman a renowned international ethnomusicologist, music is thought to be a product of the ancestors, which they use to communicate with those they like. Ambuya Rena Chitombo who at the age of 83 in 1998, was still active in music, made sure to go to bed with a book and pen that she put under the pillow and would write songs that mostly came to her in dreams.

She said, "I compose my songs through my dreams. If I dream singing, I wake up during the night and write the song," said Ambuya Chitombo who did not take dreams lightly. Before going to bed, she made sure her book and pen were under her pillow. "Dreams are very powerful because that is the way one communicates with the spiritual world."

Mbuya Chitombo also wrote some of her dreams which she later translated to real situations.

Ambuya Chitombo's musical career stated when she was at school in Mutare. When she became a school teacher, she continued with her music, also teaching school children. She joined the Bulawayo's famous choir masters at the time. She encouraged women not to stop singing once they get married.

Sylvia Sondo

O riginally from South Africa, she was a nursing sister by profession. Sylvia Sondo led the group The Yellow Blues in the 1950's. She revolutionarised the music scene by her dance as she danced to Chachacha music which is known as Rhumba today, compared to the soft dance performed by other women musicians

Sylvia came to settle in Harare after marrying Sonny Sondo, who was the leader of the 1950's City Quads band. Sylvia graced the music scene in the 1950's with an all female troupe called The Yellow Blues. They combined township jazz music with dance music mostly Rhumba music. Sylvia's shows became popular because of her unique dance unlike other women who were 'careful' about the way they carried themselves in the public. The African Daily news under the column: "Women Set The Ball of Jazz Rolling" reported:

"There was a moment, brief though it may be, in the history of Jazz-O-African Townships when women led the men. We can fix this period somewhere during 1954 to 1955. There was a memorable occasion when Vic Chingate's Gay Gaieties jointly staged a concert with another female troupe. It all happened at the Runyararo Hall. Young women leapt and wriggled in fantastic dance-styles. The Yellow Blues, although short - lived, owe their existence to the untiring energy of Mrs. Sylvia Sondo, wife of showman Sonny Sondo." (11 January 1958)

Joyce Ndoro

oyce Ndoro fronted the De Black Evening, and became the only female musician who stayed the longest with the group. She sang and performed the song Goli Goli, an Indian song which she was taught at a cultural festival in Harare. Joyce was one of the most popular women musicians of the 1950's-1960's. she also won the Miss Harare beauty title. Joyce Ndoro was one of the early township women musicians who set the Ball of Jazz rolling in the townships. Refusing to stay in the smoky kitchen, Joyce preffered to delight her fans with hectic Rhumba dances (Parade Magazine 1958). The African Daily News had this to say about Joyce Ndoro;

"Joyce made her mark with the De Black Evening Follies, as she serenaded with Jonathan Chieza. She was an active participant in furthering the cause of Townhship Music, and jazz in particular Another aspect of Joyce's life, was her glamour and alluring appearance on stage. No wonder, hundreds of Harare concert fans hailed her when she was crowned "Miss Harare 1955." (1 March 1958)

Ruth Mpisaunga

The late Ruth Mpisaunga (Muchawaya) was born in 1939 and stayed in the New Line Section of Mbare, near Mai Musodzi Hall, then Harare's hub of entertainment. She, therefore, had easy access to musical activities at the hall, and soon got involved with the "Menton and Sisters" musical group, led by Jeremiah Kainga, becoming one of the backing vocalists on his hit song *"Imi Munosara Nani Ndaenda"*.

She left music to train as a teacher and, thereafter, worked in Harare, where she got involved in drama. Ruth acted in Macbeth (Zulu version), produced and directed by Adrian Stanley in the late 50's. The play drew a lot of audiences from both blacks and whites - delighted to witness Macbeth modified into an African context. Despite the racial segregation of the day, the popular drama had mixed audience. Ruth played the part of "Nowawa", the wife of Macbeth, and Joseph Chaza played Noluju-Macbeth.

In the 70s, Ruth wrote a booklet on entertainment in the home, inspired by her exploratory experiences.

In an interview before her death she said, "I now look back to my contribution in music and the arts, and I feel fully content with the role I played."

Yes she contributed immensely in the arts and paved a way for today's women in the arts.

Date

Date

Date

Lyrics-*How Women Compose Music (Honest Lyrics fired women singers up)*

Women musicians lyrics has been to a large extent shaped by the way a woman expresses herself in her daily life. How she is supposed to behave in the public space. For women to be accepted in the public space they have to abide by certain rules and this has controlled their voice and artistic expression. As a result they are few women musicians who have composed their music 'honestly' and used music to express their feelings.

When Dorothy Masuka came into the music scene in the 50's she brought in a new era as regards women and urban music, she was using music to expressing her feelings. Although Dorothy Masuka belonged to the early urban hybrid music which was associated with the so called 'decent' or 'respectable' women who did not rock the boat and did not threaten set structures laid by society, Dorothy came and did the opposite. The lyrics of her music were very different from the ones by women like Lina Mattaka and Evelyn Juba in the 1930's. She responded to her environs without fear of being ostracized by society, she sang about shabeens, about fashion, about politics. Dorothy's lyrics reflected what was happening in society in the 50's. She sang about her true feelings and not what society wanted and expected to hear but what she wanted to communicate to society. Masuka's music sold in numbers because, society either bought the records out of curiosity or they felt they had to face the truth and dance and sing along with her. Being honest to her feelings made Dorothy one of the best composers in the history of Zimbabwe and Southern Africa, she did not allow anything to come between her voice and her artistic expression.

She became one of the best composers because she was singing from within and the words just flowed without any inhibitions and without pretence. Musicians who sing from the heart and bringing out their feelings have made a mark in the history of music as they bring in a new era or something new, something refreshing. They introduce something synonymous with them and Dorothy was one of these musicians.

Dorothy Masuka's song UNolishwa confronted society in the way they perceived a woman who wore bogarts (trousers). Masuka puts herself in the position of a man who is saying I love Nolishwa even if she puts on bogarts, I love her. Women who wore bogarts were not respected by the society, they were seen as lose women. Dorothy herself wore bogarts and is seen in many photos of the 1950's wearing this gear. In a way she was talking about herself and other women who chose to wear bogarts.

Masuka was not only a musician who was influencing fashion trends but also as an activist who through her music demystified the society's notions about women who dressed in bogarts, and giving confidence to women. The way women chose to dress has been an ongoing debate even to this day. In 1992 female students at the University of Zimbabwe held a demonstration in solidarity with women who were being beaten up for choosing to wear miniskirts and trousers.

She also sang and composed political songs and one of the most popular political songs she composed was called UMalan (Malan Ulomthetho Onzima). This song got her into trouble and she was banned from South Africa. She could not live in Zimbabwe then Rhodesia either as she was considered security threat in both countries. She went to live in Zambia in exile and only came back to Zimbabwe and South Africa when the two countries had gained independence.

Susan Chenjerayi is also one woman who made her name in music through her lyrics. In the late 1960's while the hype of music from outside Zimbabwe was going on as musicians like Dorothy Masuka had gone into exile. Susan Chenjerayi emerged on the local scene and she was to change the musical terrain with a strong Zimbabwean rhythm and songs which that had to do, mostly about the problems women were facing in early urban life. This brought many people closer to home than the music that was going on before Susan Chenjerayi came onto the scene, which was from neighouring countries. Some of her popular songs were Ndatemwa negogo, Mai Mwana Ndanyara and many others. The song Amai mwana ndanyara was about a woman who had come unannounced to her home in the township and found that there was another woman. When the wife asked who she was she was told that she was a distant relative, which was obvious that the husband was lying. When the husband realized that the wife did not believe him he apologized and said Amai mwana ndanyara (the mother of my child I am ashamed). This was brave of Susan Chenjerayi because then women could not easily challenge men but when her songs were played they became a voice for the voiceless urban women.

In the 1970's Susan Mapfumo came into the local scene and she created her public persona through her frank and blunt lyrics. One of her songs was about being divorced, which shocked the public. In this song Ndakanga ndakaroorwa ini [kwaMurehwa] (I was once married [in Murehwa]) she sang the song as she was celebrating being divorced. Instead women were supposed to stick to their marriages no matter what or if they had been divorced cover themselves in shame as women who had failed their families and society. Susan decided to change the society by challenging attitudes towards divorce. She did not want to waste her time mourning but to boost her moral by going into a celebratory mood; 'I was divorced, but life has to go on and here is my story of how I was divorced and the problems that I went through'. The rhythm of the song took listeners into a celebratory mood as well as demystifying divorce as regards women and assuring them that there was life after the break up. Mapfumo gave women a voice and confidence. She also sang a song about a man who was not bringing full pay at home and making the family to suffer Baba vaBhoyi Maita Seiko (What has happened to you the father of my children). This song went on very well with women and Susan Mapfumo in the 1970's became the spokesperson for women.

As a way of preaching and contributing to society the Two Singing Nuns surprised the society with their lyrics which also made them to become spokespersons for women. Songs which became popular were Baba ve Mwana (nditengereyiwo platform, ndiyendeseyiwo kwaMushandira Pamwe) (Please the father of my children please buy by me a shoe called platform and also please take me to the Mushandira Pamwe Night Club). The Two Singing Nuns also composed the song Baba Tipfavireyiwo (Father be kind on us) this was at the height of the war in the 1970's.

Shuvai Wutaunashe also composed a prayer song Tarira Nguva, at the height of war in 1979 she says, "I took it in so many contexts at the time that was in 1979 the war was raging and there were also families being destroyed there was so much pain everywhere. And I felt that especially Christians we should not just look at a situation and stay away. I must know that I am called into the kingdom for such and such a time like this (kingdom of God) with so much pain and so much trouble so much chaos I will do my part if I do not do it still God will bring deliverance from somebody else but if I do it God will give me honour and a blessing so that is the message and the blessing behind it".

Some young women today have followed the trend and their lyrics are to the point. It is important for women to compose honestly as this will bring out their voice and artistic expression and will be able to use music as a tool to bring about change and create their own personality in the music scene.

Women celebrate your lives in song.

Date

Bertha Mattaka-Msora

During the early days of Zimbabwe's popular music in the 1930's, women were also at the forefront, blazing a trail for the youth who were to succeed them. Bertha Mattaka-Msora was a young female musician/entertainer of the 1950's, who followed her parent's footsteps. Lina Mattaka, her mother, was a pioneer musician who confronted gender prejudice in the musical arena.

Bertha started singing at the age of five alongside her parents, and featured as a member of the Mattaka family in the musical programme; "Rufaro Mumba", produced by Ephraim Chamba in 1959, for the Federal Broadcasting Corporation (FBC). She also took part in the film: "Mattaka Buys a Bicycle," were her father was the main actor. She also appeared in a 15-20 minute film, with brother Eddison on piano. At the 1969 Neshamwari Festival, Bertha won a first prize for soprano solo. She was a playright and actress, and won an award for her play: "I Will Wait", which was sponsored by the Zimbabwe Publishing House in 1982. Bertha also wrote a script "Nyasha", a TV Series on baby dumping.

Besides her music and acting career, Bertha was an educationist, tutor and trainer.

Bertha's ambition was to re-record some of the sentimental tunes she used to sing with the family she recorded a few on the film documentary Mattaka Family directed by Joyce Jenje Makwenda (1993), were she appeared with her parents. Unfortunately she passed away in 2005.

Mabel Bingwa

The year 1953 had its uniqueness. While politicians saw the Federation become reality, socialites attended the centenary of Cecil John Rhodes. It was in Bulawayo, 22 miles away from Matopo, where they laid his remains in 1902. There were delegates of all kinds and from all nations. But it is at this time that the attention of the country became focused on "16- year old" Mabel.

The Follies were the only Rhodesian group invited to entertain people, and Mabel was with them. She sang side by side with the Manhattan Brothers, competing with Dotty Masuka and Miriam Makeba. Throughout the three weeks she remained at the Centenary City she drew large audiences to herself. She jived and mimicked the sorrows of the African reserves and townships." (25, February 1958- *The African Daily News).*

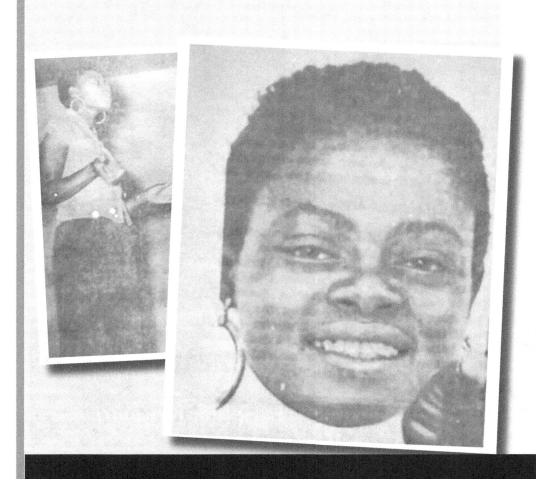

Flora "Zonk-Girl" Dick

lora was not just a simple jazz woman, but a singer of rare merit. In her mezzo-soprano voice she provided the then Rhodesia with some of the best ever recorded pieces. Listeners of the African Service of the Federal Broadcasting Corporation ranked Flora's "Sesse-ture" Highly as it captures the minds of many Zimbabweans.

...When she invaded Malawi (Nyasaland) in 1954, so enthusiastically was received that the audience still have a vivid impression of the dark Mashona jazz beauty.

Flora is to be remembered as an audacious woman who influenced the course of jazz." (25 February 1958)

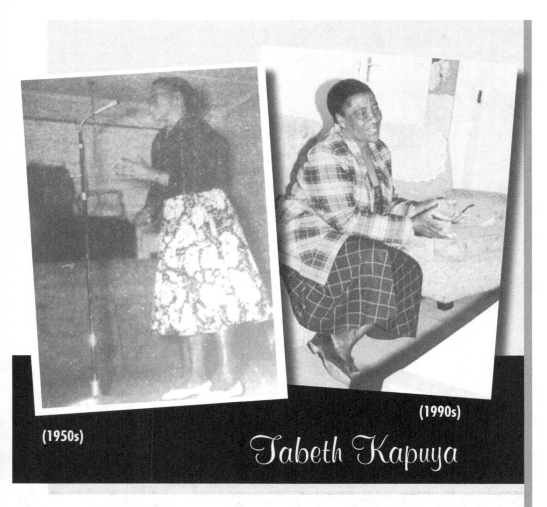

(1990s)

(1950s)

Tabeth Kapuya

Despite society's attitude towards women musicians, women in the 50s championed their own liberation in music. Tabeth Kapuya was among those courageous women who set the ball of jazz rolling in what was then Harare township. Tabeth did her apprenticeship under Victoria Chingate who was like a mother to her. She joined Gay Gaieties in 1955 when she was still at school.

"Mrs Chingati was a serious musician who wanted us to give the audience a quality show." When the Gay Gaieties disbanded, Tabeth teamed up with the Golden Rhythm Crooners and with them visited the dam site at Kariba to entertain the Italians and the Britons who were constructing the Kariba Dam.

She also teamed up with Simangaliso Tutani and composed a song, "Uri Mudiwa Wangu Iwe, Simanga" (you are my love Simanga). "Simanga helped me in my musical carreer; he taught me how to sing."

Tabeth Kapuya grew up in Mbare together with Faith "Show Gun Boogie" and Flora "Zonk Girl" Dick who were among the early women township jazz musicians.

Tabeth's wish has been to organize an all-female group and teach young people how to sing.

According to the African Daily News; "She was smallish at the time, but swift and sure-footed; the self voice characterised Tabitha Kapuya. Wherever she sang audiences would quickly recognise her unique talent. She crooned and jived to the joys and sorrows of her people. (22 March 1958)

Date

Date

Date

Grace James

Scores of African women have tramped the Rhodesian stage over the past ten years. Some played a prominent role for years, that their names will ever be remembered. Others too, in a small way, would never be overlooked. These could be classified as small time singers; such is a characterization of great stars who had a humble beginning. In this category we place Miss Grace James of the Show Down Quakers.

Over the past few months Grace has been rising high up the ladder in showbiz. Critics and concert fans have noticed in her a tremendous wealth of undeveloped talent. I was startled when I attended one of her recent concerts in Highfield. So well did she sing; her jazz style was so fine that it was all like a dream. When I heard her present "Farayi Mose", my blood warmed up. She sang it with the ease and accomplished poise of a master. Her clear soprano voice rang like a skylark on a warm summer morning.

Yes to this day Grace, together with several other African women has helped to set the Ball of Jazz Rolling in the African Townships." (19 April 1958)

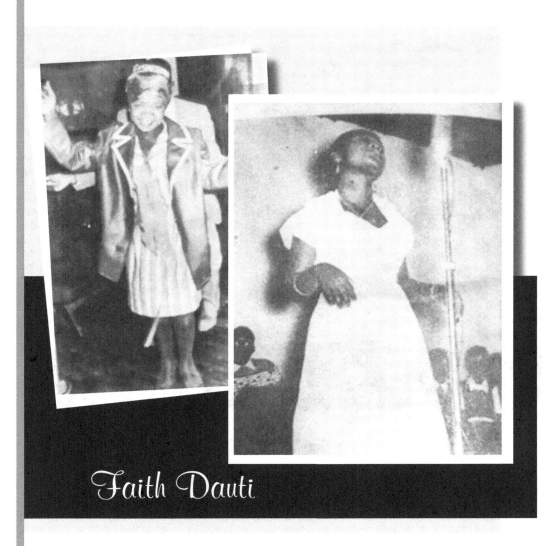

Faith Dauti

Faith Dauti was a brilliant composer and arranger, who was at times mistaken for Dorothy Masuka's sister because of the similarities of their voices. Some of the songs she composed and arranged were: Rosvika Zuva, (The Day has come) Hama neva Bereki (from the tune Hamba noNsokolo by Dorothy Masuka), Ngatipemberei, (Lets rejoice) Shoko rasvika (The Word has Come), and many others. Rosvika Zuva was played on General Service which was not usually the case as Shona songs were only played on the African Service and the General Service was meant for Europeans. This was during the General strike of the 1950's, the song was about love and the authorities used to persuade Black workers to abandon the strike and go back to work.

Faith's music was very much a fixture of the earlier 'township jazz' era, with jazz band accompaniments. Faith sang with the Milton Brothers but she also teamed up on occasion, with similar – and now legendary - groups such as the City Quads, Golden Rhythm Crooners and De Black Evening Follies. Nicknamed 'Shot Gun Boogie' after one of her trademark songs, an article in the African Daily News admiringly stated that 'Faith must have been born when the allocation of voices to creatures was still fresh!' Faith Dauti passed away in 1970.

Susan Chenjerayi

While people were still excited by music outside Zimbabwe in the 1960s, Susan Chenjerayi emerged on the local scene with a new genre that changed the musical terrain, which had a strong Zimbabwean rhythm. Her music career started in the 50's with the Bantu Actors, under the apprenticeship of Lina Mattaka and later with Sylvia Sondo's Yellow Blues.

She was a part of a duo with Safirio Madzikatire, Chenjerayi was one of the best composers and musician. Some of her songs include Isaac Hawuchandida Here? Mwedzi Muchena, Dali Iwe Ndosara Nani. She also composed Vana Amai Vanerugare (Mothers have a good life) which she unfortunately did not record, but was later recorded by Thomas Mapfumo. (Interview with Susan Chenjerayi 1995). Her music varied from what can be called mellow music to jiti.

Susan also became popular in the Mhuri YaMukadota television series first, and she was affectionately known as Amai Rwizi.Susan Chenjerayi influenced her children who were to be popular in the 1970's up to 1990's. Jane Chenjerayi rose to fame with her song Usandimirire Pagedhi which was a fusion of jiti and pop. Her other daughter, Daisy Chenjerayi, made it in the 1980's -1990's with her song Zai Regondo. Her youngest daughter Petronilla, who is now late, rose to prominence as an actor and she worked with her mother in her radio and TV productions. Her granddaughter Meylene Chenjerayi has also taken after her grandmother and mother Jane Chenjerayi.

Amai Rwizi was recently honoured by the Professional Women Executives and Business Forum (Proweb) for her role in the arts sector.

Now a born-again Christian married to Pastor Mobape, she has since moved on to evangelical work,

but is still held in high esteem by the musicians she worked with, her community and people who

Sarah Mabhokhela

ORN in 1931, she grew up in both Johannesburg and Harare. She started singing and performing in the 1950's era although Sarah Mabhokela made an impact in the 1960's when she returned to her country of birth, South Africa, where she performed with the Mahotella Queens. Sarah Mabhokela did a brilliant rearranging of Jeremiah Kainga's song *Imi Munosara Nani Ndaenda* which Jeremiah had recorded with a woman musician, Ruth Mpisaunga. Sara recorded the song with the Mahotella Queens, a Mbaqanga South African outfit and it became an instant hit. The fusing of Shona with mbaqanga music became a hit and Sarah Mabhokela went on to write more Shona songs for the group. Some of the Shona songs composed by Sarah Mabhokela were *Zvekumusha, Dai Kurikwedu Machembere*. When the Mahotella Queens, who had a large following in Zimbabwe, toured the country to perform the fusing of Shona and South African languages, it earned them popularity and an even larger crowd than before. It also became a marketing strategy for them.

Most of her songs have been re-arranged by her nephew Louis Mhlanga and has given them a new feel by singing them. Louis Mhlanga's daughter has also done her own rendition of the songs on the Women's Voices Album entitled *Women's Voices of Zimbabwe* and produced by Joyce Jenje Makwenda. Sarah Mabhokela came back to Zimbabwe in the 1980's and continued with her musical career, sometimes singing with Dorothy Masuka or her nephew Louis Mhlanga.

She passed away in 1988 at the age of 57.

Date

Date

Date

Why women opt for gospel music
Gospel Music and Women

Although the music industry is male dominated, there is one music genre which women musicians have found it easy to penetrate; Gospel music.

Many women in Zimbabwe have found Gospel music as the easiest way of getting into music; they have used Gospel music as their entry into music and for some they have used it as an exit point from the music scene.

While for some gospel music has been a true calling but for some it is a way of entering into popular music in a so called dignified way. They are women musicians who feel that for them to be accepted by the society they have to start their musical careers in church and then graduate to sing Gospel music, whilst for some, they start in popular music and retire in Gospel music.

Women musicians like Virginia Sillah –Jangano and Susan Chenjerayi-Mobape started their musical careers as popular musicians and they made names in their respective genres, but now they would like to go into Gospel music. Virginia Sillah who would like to record her music, says: "I don't think I can record my old music (township jazz), now because as it is now I've changed I want to go gospel as a born again Christian. If ever I want to record it must be gospel. I will give my daughter all my township jazz music so that she can record it as she is talented musically". Susan Chenjerayi also shares the same sentiments with Virginia Sillah as she has also become a born again Christian, she would like to record Gospel music. For Susan and Virginia Gospel music is an exit point in their musical career.

Women in church have to fight different levels of oppression. Despite women constituting a large number of the congregation, the leaders of the church are men, who are ministers, pastors, and priests. Many churches do not have women leaders, in the highest echelons. Some churches still do not believe that a woman can stand in front of the congregation and minister. The recent introduction of women as ministers in some churches has seen these churches cracking.

A woman has to be preached to, which means that the voice of women is not heard; how women would like to translate verses in the Bible, how they would like to shape their destiny in church is suppressed. Women can preach to other women particularly in the Mother's Union gatherings, which, in most churches the services are first presided upon by the priest or pastor, and then women can have their own time later. Most of the time is spent on women advising each other on how to look after the home, children and husbands.

The Church controls women's voice by using the verse in Bible, taken from 1 Corinthians 14:33-35, : "As in all the congregations of the saints, women should remain silent in the churches. They are not allowed to speak, but must be in submission, as the Law says. If they want to inquire about something, they should ask their own husbands at home; for it is disgraceful for a woman to speak in the church." The verse has been translated to strengthen patriarchal structures in the church.

Women are however needed for their singing services in the church, in most churches they constitute 95% and they even end up singing bass. This is the only voice they provide in the church and it is already controlled, by the mere fact that men control the church.

It is in the church that women are structured to be 'good women'. That is why going into the public space and singing church songs known as Gospel music is in a way seen as a way of ministering, not entertaining.

This does not provide the freedom that is needed in women's self - expression as this comes with a lot of deception that makes it difficult for women to be themselves.

Despite the controls put in place for women they have made their mark in Gospel mainstream music. In the 1970's The Two Singing Nuns shocked society by singing church music and other types of music and playing guitars.

In the 1980's Shuvai Wutaunashe brought in a unique kind of Gospel music which is fused with African praise worship. She says: " If you look in the Bible, the early church even the old church – I mean the Old Testament, this was the kind of praising............ the Bible said dance, 'Come let us clap our hands to the Lord, come let us lift our hands to the Lord and people want to be free in church. The kind of God we serve wants the people who stand before Him, free to worship him, to shout praises to his name and really praise him. I really believe from the depth of my heart that music was meant for God and with all types of instruments ...anything. And it is such a pity that we have left some of our instruments to rot, like mbira".

Since the 1990's we have seen women musicians taking Gospel music to another level. Some of the women who have made an impact in the Gospel arena are Olivia Charamba, Shingisai Siluma Fungisayi Zvakavapano and Ivy Kombo.

Although a number of women musicians chose gospel music because it is a dignified way of entering into popular music, but as they enjoy the fruits of popular music which Gospel music is part of they end up being caught up in the popular culture frenzy and they fall out of grace with society which would want to stereo type female gospel musicians. Some women musicians have fallen out of grace with society as they are seen not to be respecting gospel (church) music's 'values' because of their kind of dressing and the way they dance and behave.

A number of gospel musicians have had problems with society for not wanting to be stereo typed as gospel musicians but just as popular musicians or entertainers. It is not only the church people who come to these shows or rather who have the buying power, it is also the non church goers.

Once church music leaves the church domain going onto halls and other venues, it becomes a product of popular culture and for it to make it, it has to abide and observe the rules that make popular culture survive in the market place. Singing to an audience requires working the audience, appealing to the audience. While the musician is working the audience the audience also works the musician. To appeal to the audience a musician has to put on a costume or attire which will make her accepted or applauded by her audience. Even those who would want to see the musicians as stepping out of line, the so called conservative Christians admire the trendy kind of dressing but because of their conditioning they have to be seen to be condemning it in order to please their constituencies.

Women should continue to celebrate Gospel Music with all they have; attire, instruments, dance and voice.

Virginia Sillah

BORN in Bulawayo, Virginia Sillah ('Sisi Vee'; 'The Queen') emulated her father, David Sillah - a jazz singer/pianist. Additional encouragement came from her aunt, Ethel Jaya, who looked after Virginia as an orphan girl. Ethel was, herself, blind.

Having left school where she had been involved in music in 1965, Virginia went into "Pop and the Blues". She teamed up with the Jairos Jiri's "Sunrise Kwela Kings Band" in 1966 and, thereafter, with The Keynotes Revellers. She moved to Harare in 1969, and signed up with the OK Success.

In 1972 she joined Green Jangano and the Harare Mambos, later marrying Green. Virginia was with the outfit for 25 years, and recorded: *"Ndafunafuna"* - a tune originated by the City Quads; *"Mbuya Nehanda"* - a tune derived from a traditional lyric sung during the liberation struggle, which she rearranged with the Mambos. With her velvet voice, it became the Mambos' trade mark. With the same zeal she later recorded *"Amainini Handeyi* Kumusha".

Now retired from active performance, Virginia brightened the musical arena in difficult times, as a role model and champion of the Township Music revival, especially in the 80s.

Linda Nemarundwe-Maraire

S HE is known as a woman of many talents, she was full of good energies, and such was her personality. When she entered the room it lit! Her leadership qualities were second to none. Her understanding and appreciation of her traditional way of life made it easy for her to understand and fit in the global arena as she had something new to offer in that arena . She left a mark in whatever she laid her hands on.

She is celebrated here at home and internationally. Linda Chengeto Nemarundwe Maraire, affectionately known as Amai Chi, lifted the Zimbabwe flag in whatever she did, particularly through music. Wherever she was she took the opportunity to introduce mbira, ngoma (drumming) and marimba music.

"Most of us know Mai Chi through the music she helped bring from Zimbabwe to the United States. Many of us have taken Shona singing classes from her." Wrote Joel Lindstrom and Cathrine Heising on the Danemutande Magazine website, the couple spent some time with Mai Chi in 1993. She was proud of her heritage and she passed on the heritage to her daughter Chiwoniso Maraire who has taken Zimbabwe mbira music to a higher level. Chi, as she is affectionately known, paid tribute to her mother with the song *Mai Fambai Zvakanaka,* Mother travel well mother we will see you again.

She is a woman who created her own space regarding the playing and performing of music, the space she was comfortable with, strengthening the family set by coming up with venues which were friendly to the family arrangement. Mai Chi also teamed up with her husband Dumisani Maraire. She also trained Early Childhood Education teachers and established many early learning centers in remote and urban areas in Zimbabwe. She followed her mother's footsteps the late ambuya Nemarundwe who was a successful community developer.

Beaulah Dyoko

URING 1950's, Beaulah Dyoko, a popular mbira player, said she had been very sick for over a year when she was taken to a traditional healer by her mother, who told them that her sickness was due to a spirit medium (ancestor) that possessed her and wanted Beulah to play the mbira instrument. The ancestor had been a mbira player before he died. Because women were forbidden to play the mbira instrument, these instructions were not followed and Dyoko remained sick for another year until she herself dreamt of playing the mbira. This time her mother, believing it was a further sign, agreed to buy her one. In 1996 Dyoko told me how she was initiated by the ancestors into playing mbira. The day her mother brought her the mbira she dreamt playing a song called 'Bhuka Tiende',(Wake up and go) "When I told my mother I had dreamt this song she asked me to play it and when I did it was as if I had been playing mbira for a long time, because I played it so well that day."

When Beaulah Dyoko started playing the mbira she was healed. As a result, those in her community near Zimbabwe's border with Mozambique grudgingly accepted that in fact a woman could play the mbira. During the 1960s, Dyoko became the first woman to record mbira music. She believed that she had been chosen by the ancestors. "If it is true that the mbira instrument was supposed to be played by men only, then…. [the spirit] could have gone to Beaulah's brother or could have waited for Beaulah to have sons which she has anyway," said Dumisani Maraire (ethnomusicologist) in an interview before he passed on. "But the spirit chose to possess Beaulah."

When the country gained its independence Beulah Dyoko returned to the studio and recorded a number of albums and travelled locally and international playing mbira music. Dyoko made the mbira popular by adding guitars and taking it beyond the biras, (night vigils).

Unfortunately she passed on in May 2013.

Susan Mapfumo

SUSAN Mapfumo first surfaced as the vocalist with the OK Success Band in the early 1970s, and then went on to make many fine recordings under her own name. A 'gender activist' in the 1970s - long before most had ever heard of one – she became the voice of oppressed women. Susan was, the first woman to own musical instruments, and to lead and manage her own band.

Susan Mapfumo took the music industry by storm in the late 1970s with her song Baba Va Bhoyi, which was a mixture of Rhumba, Mbaqanga, Pop and traditional music and a bit of rock music. It was well received by the audience as it heralded a new era of a new fusion and also the strong message, which questioned the way a father was spending his money by bringing half of his pay home. During the 1970's not many African women were gainfully employed and they depended on their husbands financially as they took care of the home and children.

Many of her songs reflected an independent temperament that was unusual for African women of her time and place: 'Baba vaBhoyi' ('What has happened to you, father of my children?'); 'Kwenya Mhezi' ('Scratch your own measles/sort out your problems, man!'); and the popular 'KwaMurehwa' ('I was once married in Murehwa'). She gave a narration of how difficult it was when she was divorced but the mood the rythm of the song created was that of celebrating that she was now going on with her life, and yet women were supposed to feel ashamed when there were divorced but it was not the case with Susan Mapfumo.

Susan Mapfumo composed more than 25 songs and most of them were hits and her songs are still popular today.

Susan died at the age of forty-four in 1991. She left a legacy!

Date

Date

Date

Women Musicians and Personal Time in Zimbabwe

Women's personal time is determined by their family and society.

Patriarchy aims to confine women to the home where they do unacknowledged or unpaid work. Often they combine the responsibilities of working to earn a wage and doing all the domestic work. This unfair division of labour when girls are growing up and when they finally have their "own" homes, means that they do not have much time to spend on developing themselves and their talents. In many patriarchal societies, women are supposed to confine themselves to the domestic sphere. Their access to public space is very limited. They are not supposed to develop a public persona.

There are some women who try to fight all odds when they are still young, and fulfil their goals, but when they get to a certain age, for instance if they get married, the structures set by the society remind them that they are "women" and they give up on their dreams.

This has contributed to a large extent to women lacking personal time to continue with their aspirations.

It becomes even more difficult when a woman wants to be in a field or profession that will take her away during odd hours or for a long time away from home. Women who have chosen music as a career have had to find ways of dealing with their families or society in order for them to make it. It could be easier when they are still single but once they decide to marry and have a family it becomes a challenge.

With marriage comes the responsibility of re-arranging priorities. As a wife, she is called to put her husband's needs before her own. This often means compromising on the amount of time she spends on music, if her husband is at all interested in continuing with music.

In this day and age where women usually need to work to supplement the family income, it becomes almost impossible to be an effective wife, a good mother, a reliable employee and a great musician at the same time.

When the demanding lifestyle becomes stressful, music is often the first thing to be taken off the list. Laura Bezuidenhout an accomplished musician who has been in music since the 1970's and has been involved in music in Zimbabwe and South Africa has made the following observations as regards women musicians and personal time, "A lot of men who marry female musicians tend to become possessive and jealous after the marriage, and they often force their new wives to choose between their careers and their marriage.

Society also plays a role here — music is seen as an activity for youngsters, carefree, without responsibilities and more often than not, a little on the frivolous side.
Society expects a married woman to conduct herself as such, and the negative associations with music is often too overbearing for general societal acceptance. In the paternalistic society we live in, women are tossed from side to side when trying to chart their lives, and they are often not allowed to make the necessary decisions that will accommodate both her "talents and her in-laws", so to speak...," says Laura Bezuidenhout.

The structures of the society are designed in such a way that women find it difficult to work in the home and outside the home, this put pressure on them and they have to choose whether to continue with outside work or the home.
Usually it is the home that they have to choose as they are brought up to feel that they are obliged to make the home run smoothly and if it does not they feel they have failed the family and society.

Lina Gumboreshumba started her musical career at a young age and she had time to pursue her musical dream as she came from a musical family and she would accompany her father to play at bira's (night vigils). She has taken music to another level and she now has a Master's in Music, which she teaches and also works for the Hugh Tracy Library.
While she has been one of the lucky few women musicians who have fulfilled their aspirations she feels that the requirements of music and marriage often clash, "I think the demands of a musical career and the demands of marriage for a woman as expected by the husband and the society at large clash.

Being a musician demands many hours of practising, and some performances are done outside the "normal" day hours, as a result many men are not comfortable with their wives tackling the heavy schedule and working odd hours. The demands of the family weigh down on the woman and in the end she has to make a choice and drop the other. So married women musicians really need their husbands' and families' support for their career to succeed," says Lina Gumboreshumba.

Despite the structures of the society which has made it impossible for women to fulfill their aspiration from an early age to adulthood, some women musicians have learnt how to create time in order to have their place in the music scene.

When Prudence Katomeni-Mbofana one of the best Jazz musician and a renowned actor was asked to be part of a musical play while she was breastfeeding her second child says the show was a success and even the producer did not know how she was able to do it as she would breastfeed her child just before going onto the stage. She created time for the play to be successful.

Prudence Katomeni-Mbofana's career started at an early age while she was at high school and she seems to be going stronger, despite being a mother and a wife. She also gets support from her husband Comfort Mbofana.

Tambudzayi Hwaramba, who made her name in the urban grooves genre in the 90's, was involved in music from a tender age and she managed to do this by creating personal time to accommodate her music in whatever she did, "I've always had a passion for song and dance. When I was in primary school I used to invite my friends over to my house for singing and dancing competitions. We would compete to see who could sing popular songs by musicians like Yvonne Chaka Chaka best.

"Of course, I would practise all week so that I could know every song by heart. I would watch all the music programmes on TV and imitate the dances and performances. At this stage, I just thought I enjoyed music but didn't realise that God had given me a particular gift. I didn't even realise that there was potential for creativity in me."

Tambudzayi continued with her music when she went to secondary school. "I went to High School (Arundel Girls High School). However, this was when I became aware of the fact that I had a God-given talent. I met a girl called Dumisani Nkala who was a brilliant piano-player.

We became friends and we would sit together in one of the school piano rooms while she practiced. As time went on and as we got comfortable around each other, we began singing together and writing songs together. By the time we were in our second last year of High School, Dumi and I were part of an all-girls gospel band called Milele.

Other members of the band included Farirai Mukonoweshuro, Ratidzai Magura and Nyaradzo Ngwerume. Milele performed at a few concerts in their time" Says Tambudzayi as she goes back in time.

Nyasha Bare, who is one of the few women musicians to enrol in music education in the late 80's, realised her music talent when she was young and since then she has not looked back.

She now teaches music and she has also recorded a Gospel album. "I had interest in music from a very young age up to when I started my primary education. I used to participate in school choirs and traditional dance groups and when I went to secondary school, I was a choir leader for Sunday school and I also used to conduct a school choir at boarding school.

After my secondary school education I went to Chivhu where I was a temporary choir mistress for six years. My choir used to come out number one or two."

Stella Chiweshe, the Queen of Zimbabwe Mbira Music, realising that she had musical talent learnt to multi task while working, "When I was a child I used to herd cattle with my grandfather.

"As you obviously know cattle are herded so far from the house, from there I'd sing my voice loud so that people at the house would hear my voice.

"So when I got home (those days) my mind and body would form a rhythm which I still have up to this day. I would play the rhythm even on plates, the tables — anything that would give me sound."

The late Elizabeth Ncube, the first female Imbongi, was not all that lucky when she started her musical career as she was always reminded of housework and that as a woman she should stay at home.

Although she resisted this kind of treatment and she followed her heart she became the first female Imbongi and her parents were impressed.

In an interview that I had with her in the early 90's, she said "I knew I was going to perform but I did not know what to say to my parents it was difficult for me to tell them as they used to say a woman must not be exposed too much to the outside world (umuntu wesifazana kumele ahlale pansi).

A woman was not supposed to go to a beerhall, a woman was just supposed to look after children at home. Sweep the house etc. But then what I had was too powerful for me. My parents were now the ones asking me when next was I going to perform?"

Shuvai Wutaunashe, a celebrated Gospel musician since the late 70's, encourages women to create time in order for them to be able to make it in the music industry.

"It takes effort and a woman has to be able to divide her time. Because I am a married woman, I am a wife and I have two children.

"There are the things I take seriously and am fortunate that my family supports me. A woman in my position needs to have time and at the same time working."

Women create personal time in order to fulfill your aspirations, as you continue to celebrate womanhood.

Date

Jane Chenjerayi

JANE Chenjerayi followed in her mother's footsteps, Susan, she rocked the musical scene in the 70's. Her song Usandimirire Pagedhi was on top of the charts and it went on to number one in 1977; a traditional song which was sung by young people when the moon had settled, based on a traditional song, it relates to an old belief that certain positions of the moon determine the ideal time to look for one's life partner. Jane Chenjeray turned it into pop music and it went down very well with the township teenagers then.

Jane's carreer started in 1972 when she was still at school, she was inspired by her mother who used to rehearse with her band at home. She started with the Pied Pipers, then she joined the Wagon Wheels which was led by Oliver Mutukudzi, she also had a stint with the Green Arrows, at one time she also teamed up with Elisha Josamu.

Like any other youngster of the 70's Jane Chenjerayi started by playing, Soul, Blues, Rock and Pop. She used to sing with Choas Mudoka, Tendai, Fungayi and Gideon Neganje. She moved from copyrights and graduated into Afro Pop composing her own songs.

She joined the two guys who used to rehearse with her mother; Jack Maravanyika and Norman Neganje, she also sang with the Pied Pipers.

She left the Pied Pipers in 1977 and she recorded her first song *Usandimirire Pagedhi*, with The Wagon Wheels, and Oliver Mtukudzi. Besides *Usandimirire Pagedhi,* she also recorded, *Anzwadzi Yangu, Murume Wangu uneshanje,* which she did with Crispen Matema which was her last recording.

Besides singing she is was also an actor, and was featured in the Mukadota Family, she was one amai Musinja Kamwe the African Doctor. She was also a cover girl for magazines.

The Two Singing Nuns

THE Two Singing Nuns took the music industry by surprise as they sang songs about the emancipation of women and political music in riddles. The Two Singing Nuns were the now late Sister Tendayi Helen Maminimini and Gertrude Matsika now Mrs Mushayabasa. Their most popular songs were Tatetereka (We have wondered [in the bush]), this was during the war, Kundenderedzana (a married man wondering aimlessly with other women). Their songs went on to top ten and up until now they are still popular. Of course, the public were always curious and questioned what made the nuns sing marriage-related tunes!'

They recorded briefly for Teal Records in the mid-1970s but the quality of their output was very high and their records sold well. The two nuns who sang to great popular acclaim while accompanying themselves on guitars changed public attitudes towards that instrument from the earlier era of female public performances.

Their songs were accompanied by two guitars bass and lead and they sang in Shona. The Two Singing Nuns, who became very popular guitarists in the 1970's, learnt how to play the instruments when they were at university, and by that time they were novices. A friend, who was also a nun, taught the two how to play the guitar. They created time in between studying for their degrees.

Sister Getrude Matsika later decided to get married. She however continued to sing and play the guitar, and taught music at the school where she was also the Head. Both nuns, at some point, had to stop actively playing the guitar and being involved in music in the public space. Sister Helen Maminimini, before her tragic death, was the Order Superior–General of The Little Children of the Blessed Lady (LCBL) General and, because of the duties that she had to perform, she could not be involved in music as before.

Laura Bezuidenhout

LAURA Bezuidenhout, a white young woman, who belonged to an outfit called the Movement, was seen in the black townships with Movement Band, visiting their homes and even playing at Mushandira Pamwe which was a nightclub in the black township of Highfields. She played the piano and was the only woman in the band. The Movement Band became one of the multiracial bands which had a composition of almost all the ethnic groups in Zimbabwe, and because of that it got a wide following. The group helped her understand a number of things regarding performance and working with men: "Movement was my very own personalised seven-year "apprenticeship" in music, and my first introduction to contemporary African music, which has remained my specialty ever since.

Laura did not have support from her parents, as far as performing music in public is concerned. They felt it was insecure, "….Actually, it is a miracle that I ever discovered the musician in me. Even now, I struggle against that ingrained upbringing every day, to free my artistic self….."

It is extremely difficult for a female musician to obtain the necessary resources to launch, maintain and develop her chosen career. Laura attributes her ability to earn respect on the music scene to the resources she has had since childhood, compared to black women, but still had to subsidise her musical career with a side job.

Women who have access to resources such as musical instruments have more time to spend with the instrument, perfecting their skills. Laura was also fortunate to get proper skills through an institution. This helped to ground her into the instrument, and also to understand the theatrical aspects of the instrument.

Laura believes that society has let women musicians down, and feels other women musicians can open doors for younger musicians.

Rhoda Mandaza

An all-round artist Rhoda Mandaza has been in the music scene since the 1970's, as a singer, promoter and producer of music documentaries and videos. In most of the projects that she does music is central.

Rhoda Mandaza has had problems in some of her projects by involving men as a way of seeking validation. The men have ended up taking over the projects. She says this has blocked access for women from sustaining themselves economically. The men end up being the owners of the project, involving even more men along the way, in the end as a woman, ends up invisible. Rhoda says that in one of her projects, she had planned that women would supply food at the venue as a way of empowering women who are in the food industry. The men that she had involved ended up bringing their own food, purchased from the established food industry.

Rhoda advises women in the music industry to understand contracts, and know how to draft contracts, so that they can be covered in situations of misunderstanding with business partners. The understanding of how the music business is run is also very critical: "When going into partnerships, women should set out parameters and understand what it is the other partner is bringing. One must know how much percentage they are bringing and how everything is going to be divided, in percentages, with what you will also be bringing. Women should not be afraid to ask from the beginning how they are going to share – who owns what at the end of the day. And have a contract, even if it is sometimes embarrassing to ask a friend as this was the case with me, since I looked up to the person I had involved in my music venture as a friend."

Date

Date

Date

Zimbabwe Women:
Selective, But Effective Artistes

WOMEN musicians are more aligned, involved or have full control of certain music genres and styles than others because of certain factors that influence the particular genres and styles.

Women musicians are more into the following styles and genres — jazz, pop, rhumba, urban grooves and gospel music. Not many women are associated with rock, pennywhistle music and omasiganda (one man band) and sungura music.

Women find it difficult to be associated with certain music genres because of how the genres and styles came into being; for instance jazz music — is seen to be decent music and is associated with African American music.

When it was transported back to Africa through different mediums — radio, records and film — it found its way in the hearts of Africans who had settled in urban centres and had left their traditional homes to look for jobs in this alien and newly-found cold city.

Gibson Mandishona, who grew up in the township, explained in his foreword for the Zimbabwe Township Music Book.
He wrote, "Over the years, Zimbabwe Township Music artists have experimented, improvised and sung their way with ecstatic tunes that proved irresistible and unforgettable.

"The music nurtured a new identity which outwitted urban boredom, ushered in family entertainment, and finally bridged the middle passage between the generations of jazz/blues lovers. "Alike politicians during the colonial period, Zimbabwean musicians braved their way forward, despite being subjected to overt and covert racism, which was then a grim reality, but which nevertheless created an innovative and sleek idiom-jazz expression."

The similarities that African American and Black Zimbabweans had, contributed and encouraged Zimbabweans to use Negro Spirituals, jazz in their repertoire during their 1930s early urban music. The music's lyrics were translated into Shona or Ndebele to give it a local flavour.

Jazz music was associated with decent women and women who were part of the music were seen by society as women who maintained their dignity. Women musicians who were associated with this type of music were Lina and Evelyn and had a strong church background.

Women musicians in the 1930s started to copy other women jazz musicians and also Negro spirituals and came up with their own form of jazz; township jazz music, the women were seen as well-mannered and they became accepted by the society as civilised.

Jazz music was also used to air their grievances; it became the symbol of identity.
A musician like Dorothy Masuka sang township jazz music as protest music which resulted in her living in exile. Although Dorothy Masuka is known for jazz music, one day she surprised many and sang a rock song when she performed at the Royal Order of Zimbabwe, where great statesmen were honoured.

I thought I was not seeing properly but it was her; Dorothy Masuka singing a rock song, it must have been always in her mind and one-day it was waiting to explode. Rock music came into mainstream music to challenge the status quo, and she was with her peers, the like of Kenneth Kaunda and she must have gone back in time, and rock music would express what she felt then.

Rock music was and it is still not associated with women musicians in Zimbabwe because of how it was formed. Very few women could be said to have been associated with rock music; Susan Mapfumo and Laura Bezuidenhout are some of the few. Susan's music borrowed a lot from rock music and other types of music and Laura was the only woman who belonged to a rock outfit in the 1970's.

Rock music became popular in the 1970's, although it can be traced from the 1950's-60's under different styles; rock in roll, rock, hard rock etc. In the 1970's, it was known as hard rock and was mostly challenging the status quo, from religion, education, dressing etc. It was protest music which did not have anything to do with diplomacy as jazz would, because it did not observe society's structures as its main purpose was to change laid rules and thinking.

There were groups like Wells Fargo and Eye of Liberty in the 1970's and internationally there were groups like Chicago, Lady Zepelin, Deep Purple, the list is endless. Internationally, not many women are involved in Rock music, some of them are Tina Turner, remember Night Bush City Limits it remains one of my most favourite song in my collection.

Rock music could be classified as radical music, and women found it difficult to be associated with this kind of music as this could make it even more difficult for them to be accepted by the community/society since being in music even through the genres that are associated with women, for instance jazz, gospel etc, women still have to trade consciously.

Women would want to air their grievances in a civilised manner and also to entertain in a way that would make society accept them; jazz music is one genre that has provided them with that and gives them "dignity".

Most women are not wired for rock music in Zimbabwe and yet the way women used music in pasichigare (before colonial era) could be in a way associated with rock music were women would really express themselves, and vent out their feelings in a song, just like the way Susan Mapfumo used to.

Women in the olden days would complain to their husbands' families about their husband non performance in the main room and about their broken cooking sticks and backs and the family would attend to the problem so that the couple would have a happy life.

This was taken seriously as it was the corner stone of a happy marriage.

In today's "civilised" world women's expression is controlled by many factors which make it difficult for them to express themselves.

Omasiganda music, which is loosely known as one-man band music as the musician singing also plays the guitar, has not really found its way to women musicians.

There are few women who are into one woman musician's music and one who really made her mark in this genre was Patricia Matongo.

The solo or one-man band musicians sang and entertained township folk in the streets since the 1940's. "Omasiganda" is derived from an Afrikaans word for musician "musiciaant".

Because they performed mostly in the open, patrons paid very little for the entertainment.
Token money was often thrown to them by the enthusiastic audience.

Josaya Hadebe was one of the most famous "masiganda", his favourite tunes tended to be derogatory or vulgar in meaning. A song like, Pendeka (Prostitute), is typical of Josaya's compositions. Some tunes were satirical on women, although nevertheless, he was popular with females. Although Patricia Matongo became popular as a one woman band musician her music was laid back and was not blue like Josaya Hadebe's.

Sungura is also a music genre which seems not to attract women musicians, this could be as a result of how the music originated. Of late we have seen some female dancing groups like Amavithikazi, Mambokadzi and Girls La Musica, the women dancing groups enjoy their autonomy as women and do not necessarily belong to any male group. By so doing they are able to have control of the genre and are independent as women.

They sometimes back up the sungura groups but on hired basis, which gives them autonomy of the music and their creativity, unlike if they were permanently part of the band.
Women who are into sungura music have not recorded the music as men have done, but are more into performing the music.

"Kwela" or Pennywhistle music is one music genre which has not really been associated with women playing the instrument except providing dancing as backing.

The way the music started also makes it not attractive to women playing the pennywhistle instrument which produces what can be loosely called kwela music.

"Kwela" music once had a big following in Zimbabwe from the 1950's-1960's.

It was originally played on penny whistles, (wind instrument) and it can be traced from the black South African Townships.

The pioneers of Kwela would play in city street corners attracting both black and white passersby. The police disliked such gatherings in the city, which soon put the audience on the alert.

The sight of police automatically triggered the dispersal of the audience. "Kwela" was originally associated with social outcasts who played cards on street corners, where crowds would gather around.

At the sight of police people shouted "Kwela — Kwela", which in Zulu means "climb". The policemen would order those arrested to "climb" into police trucks, shouting "Kwela — Kwela".

The word subsequently became a warning signal at the sight of police vans, for people to flee to safety.

"Kwela" music did not initially appeal to township jazz musicians, who felt superior to pennywhistlers.
That is also how women in jazz music viewed Kwela music as unsophisticated music and they did not want to be part of it.

Kwela music was revived in the 1980's just like jazz music but it still remained a male domain, Kwela musicians are performing on a small scale, but it is still a domain for male musicians.

A project is underway to encourage young women musicians to play the penywhistle (kwela music), and other wind instruments.

Women were not part of the movement that was associated with pennywhistle music that is why up to this day the music has remained male music.

Despite not being part of some of the music genres/styles, women musicians have done well in the particular genres/styles that they have decided to be associated or be part of or take full control of.

Date

Shuvai Wutaunashe

Shuvai Wutaunashe brought in a refreshing kind of gospel music, which was a mixture of pop, jazz and traditional music. She had started her music career in 1979 and her music was influenced by the 70's and 80's music to create her own type of gospel music. Her song MuKristu went on the top of the charts and it got good coverage on air.

She transformed Gospel music from the confines of the church into popular music and made it appealing to almost everyone - whether in church or not. Many listeners have confirmed getting over their problems through her music.

Shuvai's parents were singers, and that was the basis of her love for music – from when she was still very young. Through music Shuvai met her husband, Jonathan, while studying at university - and formed the Family Singers. Jonathan taught and encouraged her to write songs. Shuvai's first composition was "Tarira Nguva" – inspired by the liberation war that was raging, with families being destroyed - causing pain everywhere.

Composed in the late 70's as a cry to God to deliver, but recorded in the early 80's, the song was on Top Ten for a long time and, up to this day, goes down as one of the best Gospel songs to come from Zimbabwe. Many other hits followed thereafter.

Shuvai, who plays the guitar and piano, encourages the use of all types of instruments in church. She encourages other women musicians to play instruments and that they should set aside time to learn instruments, she believes in women also ministering in church.

Her two children are also part of the Family Singers. Shuvai and her family own the Shelter Studios recording company.

"It takes an effort and a woman has to be able to divide her time. I am fortunate that my family supports me", says Shuvai.

Ava Rodgers

$\mathcal{I}$NSPIRED by vocalists of Faith Dauti's era and appreciating the wonderful Township tunes, the multi-talented Ava Rodgers was, however, brought up in Arcadia - a middle–class suburb reserved for people of mixed race. Born in 1952, of a father who also played Township Music, Ava made her first stage appearance at the age of three, played the piano at the age of eleven and, after school. She trained as a teacher - specialising in music.

Soon after college Ava got involved with the Reps Theatre and produced a musical, 'Motown' - which was quite unique; and another hit, 'Soul Train'. During 1978-79 she featured in a high-flying production, 'Svikiro', by Arthur Chipunza. During the same period, she starred in a musical drama, 'Rock and Revolution', by Margarita Bouzanis - which caused a stir in parliament.
In 1989 Ava became the first black conductor of the junior combined schools choirs.
Always a first, she was a pioneer black woman musical director at Reps Theatre. Ava featured prominently at Jazz festivals in Zimbabwe, including the 2002 National Hunger Concert, and has performed with a variety of local musicians - including Chris Chabuka, from whom she learnt a lot. Ava looks forward to the opportunity to play with the Cool Crooners. Her style is that of the 50's and intends to record the old 'good-times' tunes of the Township Music era, which she feels is part of her cultural identity that bestows upon her - a sense of belonging. She still finds time to train young ladies in refined stage etiquette.

Biddy Partridge

BIDDY Patridge's musical career had its origins in South Africa. She first understood Afro-jazz when she accompanied her father to a Brotherhood of Breath concert. "I thought, I saw how it works all the musicians are in conversation with each other, and the solos are about someone having a lot to say". This was her first taste of Afro-jazz, which was a breath taking experience.

Listening to Abdullah Ibrahim, Hugh Masekela and Letta Mbulu in the 70's, further spurred her love for Afro Jazz, and her upbringing in "white suburbs" - as opposed to the 'Townships' - did not deter her.

Whilst in South Africa in 1980, a playwright Matsemela Manaka lent her a saxophone, until her father donated one. She enrolled at Federated Union of Black Artists (FUBA), to consolidate her passion for music. Apart from casual gigs, the students participated in practical shows.

In Zimbabwe, her other home, Biddy was one of the few to revive Township Music. With Mhepo she was involved in the rebirth, and countrywide craze for Afro-jazz.

Mhepo was formed in the early 80's. Biddy (trumpet and keyboards) and Nigel Samuels (leader, trumpet and keyboards), were part of the group's line-up - which also included Penny Yon and Tsitsi Vera. The group disbanded in 1999 and Biddy moved to London.

Biddy returned to launch the album "Mapapiro" in Harare in 2001, with former Mhepo members. In 2002 she was involved with UK-based Zimbabweans and formed a group, Pamwechete, which included Bryan Paul, Paul Lunga, Grant Hannan and Tich Makhalisa. They developed a professional programme of Zimbabwean compositions which featured prominently at the London Africa Centre. Biddy's dream is for a full Mhepo revival - orchestrating Township Music.

In London she is involved in various music/educational projects, and promotional work on arts, jazz and photography.

Penny Yon

PENNY Yon has contributed to music as performer and promoter. She joined Mhepo in 1996, she stayed with the group for four years as the bassist. In 1995 she saw herself at the helm of putting many jazz musicians on the map, which also dispelled the myth that jazz was an old people's affair. "Young people got to realise that jazz is funky, jazz is party music," said Penny.

Besides Mhepo, Penny performed with Big Sister, an all- female group. Big Sister was a hit once upon a time.

Penny is one of the few women instrumentalists, she managed to learn how to play piano and the guitar because of the time that she was allowed to freely learn and experiment when she was growing up. She was not forced to cook like what was expected of other girls. Her parents encouraged her to take up music, and did what they could to see to it that she realised her dream. She is always grateful to her parents, who nurtured her musical talent.

"When I was ten years my mother bought me a guitar, acoustic - which I still have - from a second hand shop, $17, 00! It was a lot of money then. My father used to listen to my piano when I was learning, I used to spend at least one hour on the piano. When other kids were doing their cooking with their mums in the kitchen, preparing supper, I was on my piano."

But like many women musicians, Penny had to leave music for a while to look after her growing family. However, she came back to it and is contributing to music in many ways. She has been at the helm of a project, which encourages upcoming women musicians, called FLAME (Female Literary Arts & Music Enterprise), with Pamberi Trust.

Date

Date

WOMEN MUSICIANS OF ZIMBABWE

Date

Zimbabwe:
Women De-Mystify Mbira Music

ZIMBABWEAN traditional women musicians have made a name for themselves in the arts, despite "modern" patriarchally-structured society. The socially constructed patriarchal structures have made it difficult for women to enjoy the cultural space and create their own niche. But through this orchestrated confusion the women musicians have made great strides and are ambassadors of Zimbabwean music to the outside world.

Through dreams, ancestors have played an important role in enabling women to have their space in traditional-popular music.

It is important to understand the mystification that surrounds gender and patriarchy in traditional-popular music, especially gender and spiritual beliefs.

Traditional instruments and performance have been surrounded by myths that exclude women. The spirituality and sacredness of traditional instruments and performance has been used as a way to stop women from participating in traditional music because women are supposedly unclean.

The excuse of lack of purity is undermined by messages coming from the spirits who suggest that they want women to play mbira. Such incidents exemplify a struggle between the spiritual world and earthly patriarchal society.

Women musicians overcame patriarchal rule by using the strength that comes from the spiritual world. The ancestors provide an open door for some women. Women have entered the sphere of traditional-popular music using various channels and guides. Dreams have been a particularly strong force of inspiration that has pulled women towards traditional performance against human patriarchal rule that has tried to stop them. Dreams are a strong force in the spiritual world as they are one of the ways ancestors communicate with the living.

According to Veit Erlman, a renowned international ethnomusicologist, music is thought to be a product that the ancestors communicate, through dreams, to those whom they like.

Ambuya Rena Chitombo, who at the age of 83 in 1998 was still active in music, would make sure that when going to bed she had a book and pen under the pillow as most of her songs came through dreams.

She said: "Dreams are very powerful because that is the way one communicates with the spiritual world."

In Zimbabwe ancestors who reveal themselves to traditional women musicians through dreams, want to continue the tradition of the music they played before they died.

They played music for different purposes. It was dreams that allowed the first woman in recent times to become a well-known mbira player.

During the 1950's, Beaulah Dyoko, had been very sick for more than a year when she was taken to a traditional healer. The healer said the young girl was possessed by an ancestor who had played the mbira and wanted her to play the instrument. But because women were forbidden to play the mbira, these instructions were not followed and Beulah remained sick for another year until she herself dreamt of playing the mbira.

This time her mother, believing it was a further sign, agreed to buy her one.

In 1996 Dyoko told me how she was initiated by the ancestors into playing mbira.
The day her mother brought her the mbira she dreamt of playing a song called 'Buka Tiende' (Wake up and go). "When I told my mother I had dreamt this song she asked me to play it and when I did it was as if I had been playing mbira for a long time because I played it so well that day," she said.

When Beaulah started playing the mbira she was healed.

As a result, those in her community near the border with Mozambique grudgingly accepted that a woman could play the mbira. During the 1960s, Dyoko became the first woman to record mbira music. She had been chosen by the ancestors.

"If it is true that the mbira instrument was supposed to be played by men only, then . . . (the spirit) could have gone to Beaulah's brother or could have waited for Beaulah to have sons which she has anyway," said Dumisani Maraire (ethnomusicologist) in an interview before he passed on. "But the spirit chose to possess Beaulah."

Beaulah returned to the studio later and Stella Chiweshe, now known internationally as the mbira queen, came onto the scene.

Chiweshe had also learned to play mbira after a dream. Her mother dreamt being told that she had to teach all her children to play mbira.

But while her brothers easily found teachers, no one wanted to teach Stella until an uncle came to her rescue. She excelled far beyond her siblings. This was in keeping with the Shona belief that not everyone can learn to play the mbira, some are simply born to play while others are not. In 1974, Chiweshe recorded her first single "Kasahwa." It became a hit and was followed by 24 singles over the next six years.

Chiweshe and Dyoko made the mbira popular by adding guitars and taking it beyond the biras, (night vigils). Soon they were no longer just considered women who play the mbira but among the best African musicians worldwide.

Their powerful female influence on this instrument laid the path for the next generation of women to make their own mark on the mbira. It is also through dreams that Zimbabwe saw its first and only female imbongi (praise poet) Elizabeth Ncube. Elizabeth also was sick of an incurable illness.

When the family had tried everything to treat the illness she had a dream in which she was shown what her ancestors wanted her to do -- to be an imbongi. It was through her grandfather's spirit that Elizabeth became an imbongi when she was eleven in 1974.

Her grandfather, Mtetwa, had been an imbongi for Mzilikazi, the Ndebele king who led the Ndebele people into Zimbabwe after battles with the Zulu King Shaka in South Africa. Elizabeth had a dream in which she was wearing clothes which her grandfather used to wear, and it was these clothes that she used when performing. Ncube's choice was not easily fulfilled, she was nearly killed by a male imbongi at a competition in Harare. He tried to attack Ncube with a spear as she was performing, but Ncube overpowered the man. She attributed her ability to overpower the men to her warrior spirit.

At this competition Ncube beat the two men, including her attacker. When Elizabeth met the man some months later and confronted him about why he wanted to kill her, the man said "Wake wabona ngaphi umfazi otanyula inyawo pambili kwabantu!"("Where did you see a woman who opens her legs in front of people!")

The use of praise poetry in the Ndebele culture was fundamentally political.It was meant to sing praises or warn the head of state and also to praise fighters when they left as well as when they returned from war.

Albert Nyathi, a famous Zimbabwean imbongi attributes the lack of female imbongi to the limitations that women face because they had children and therefore could not go to war. It was the duty of the imbongi to go to war and to give moral support to the soldiers through praise poetry. However, since women were also involved in the Zimbabwe liberation struggle in the 1970's, it became appropriate for them also to be involved in the art of imbongi.

Elizabeth Ncube started her imbongi performances at political gatherings and she performed to give the cadres moral support in the camps.

Zimbabwe's liberation war was another form of authority that was able to partially override petty patriarchal rules. Although in the 1890's a woman like Mbuya Charwe, the medium of the Nehanda Spirit, had fought the British, the role of women in war had been forgotten or downplayed for decades.

However, women were to resurface as freedom fighters during the liberation struggle and they took their place in the political arena.

Mbuya Nehanda's spirit played an important role in guiding the cadres and in ensuring that women mbira players could also become important during the war.

Irene Chigamba also played for freedom fighters during the 1970's, as did Stella Chiweshe.

Another challenge to the belief that women could not or shall not play mbira came from non-patriarchal men who argued logically against such beliefs.

For instance, Dumisani Maraire, who introduced mbira to the American West Coast in the 1960's, strongly disputed the notion that mbira is not supposed to be played by women. He argued that he himself played the mbira because of his great grandmother. During an interview in 1999, he said that if women were not allowed to play mbira in pasichigare (pre-colonial period), then his grandmother and other women could not have played the instrument.

Maraire also encouraged his daughter Chiwoniso to play the mbira and Chiwonsio was known in Zimbabwe and internationally as one of the country's best mbira players.

Chiwoniso Maraire further revolutionised mbira by adding English lyrics and church songs.It was a natural choice for Chii, as she was affectionately known.

She was born in Washington State, the United States, where her Zimbabwean parents were studying and teaching mbira. Chiwoniso started playing mbira at the age of four and at 12 she was performing with her parents on stage.
Chiwoniso has won many musical awards.

Similarly, Irene Chigamba plays mbira with her father, which has not gone down well with hard core traditionalists.When Chigamba started playing mbira she was discouraged by relatives but her parents stood by her.

The most sacred and highly respected musical functions of the Shona (mbira) and Ndebele imbongi, were passed on to women by their ancestors.

Ancestors chose whom they wanted to continue with their tradition.

Date

Angela Greenland

On a career spanning 23 years Anjii has fronted some of Zimbabwe's well-loved soul, jazz, and rock bands.

She began her career singing lead professionally at the age of 16 with "Boykie" Moore and the band Colour. Performing Soul and R 'n B in venues all over Zimbabwe and opening at Rufaro Stadium for the Incomparable Staple Singers. When Colour disbanded in 1988 she joined Harare's Rock scene singing lead in the band Loaded Dice for two years. At this time she also did extensive studio work with Henry Peters and Shed Studios. In 1991 she Joined the Iconic band Sabuku, which grew out of the legendary band 'Soul and Blues Union' popularly known as SABU. In 1994 she left Zimbabwe travelling between Denmark, and England for over three years performing in various clubs and working as a session musician.

Upon her return to Zimbabwe she once again teamed up with Bryan Paul, one of Zimbabwe's most respected Bassists, who led the Jazz band Savannah Cruz. Comprising of Bryan on Bass, Sam Mataure on drums, Ritchie Lopez on Sax, Filbert Murova on Keybords and Anjii once again Lead vocals.

Anji has been recently involved in the project FLAME (Female Literary Arts & Music Enterprise) which is led by Penny Yon. Flame is a Pamberi Trust Gender Mainstreaming project, which is designed to provide a special platform for emerging women artists, to paly their music in the safety of daytime performances. Anji has been part of the "SISTAZ OPEN MIC" to give support to the young women support by performing and sharing the stage with them.

Stella Chiweshe

When Zimbabwe attained its independence in 1980, so did mbira playing. Stella Chiweshe, now known internationally as the Mbira Queen of Zimbabwe came onto the scene, like Dyoko returned to the studio. Chiweshe had also learned to play mbira after a dream. She said her mother had dreamt being told that she had to teach all her children to play mbira. But while her brothers easily found people to teach them, no one wanted to teach Stella until an uncle Gwanzura Gumboreshumba volunteered and she excelled far beyond her siblings. This was in keeping with the Shona belief that not everyone can learn to play the mbira; some are simply born to play, while others are not.

In 1974, Chiweshe recorded her first single, *"Kasahwa."* It became a hit and was followed by 24 singles over the next six years. In 1985, she formed her highly successful band, Earthquake. In early 1998, Chiweshe was one of three women showcased on the Global Divas tour, which toured all over the U.S. In the early 1980's, Chiweshe made the mbira popular by adding guitars and taking it beyond the *biras,* (night vigils). Soon she was no longer just considered a woman who played the mbira, but among the best African musicians worldwide.

Francisca Muchena

ai Muchena, as she is affectionately known, is a confident woman. I attended performances where she was singing with her husband in the 1990's, and she would just take over the stage and perform. Her husband was not worried: rather, he would support his wife. Watching their show one could see and feel a positive energy around them. In such a situation, inhibiting public space is not heavy for the women involved and they can show their musical talents without inhibitions. As Mai Muchena recounts:

"I got married in 1963, it did not bother him [my (late) husband] that I was a mbira player because we met at a bira (night vigil). He was a mbira player. I was also good at singing. He got attracted to me because of that. From there on we sang together with my husband and family. I do not play mbira that much, but the talent that I have is in playing drums, I can also play rattles, I can dance, sing even when we have gone overseas. I am the one, who usually does most of the stuff, playing drums is my specialty." (Int. 1992).

There are times when Mai Muchena would be invited to perform on her own without her late husband, and the husband did not see any problem with that. However, most couples that perform together end up fighting for attention and fame and, in cases where Mai Muchena was invited to perform alone; it could have caused problems in their marriage. Mai Muchena thinks it is a misunderstanding on the part of those husbands.

Mai Muchena would like to encourage women not to abandon their musical career because of marriage, "Women should find ways to communicate with their husbands and show that they are serious about their musical career."

Elizabeth Ncube

It was through her grandfather's spirit that Elizabeth Ncube became an 'Imbongi' (praise poet), at age eleven, in 1974. Her grandfather, Mtetwa, was an Imbongi for Mzilikazi - the king of the Ndebele people - who led his people into Zimbabwe from South Africa, after battles with Tshaka, the Zulu king.

Elizabeth had to make the society, and her own family, understand, after she had been ill for a long time, and after a dream, she was shown how to become an Imbongi. She used to dream wearing the clothes which her grandfather used to wear - the very clothes she was to use when performing: the indlhukula (hat) for amaqawe (warriors); white cloth - for a sangoma (traditional healer), because her grandfather was one; a red cloth which she wrapped around her waistline - for hunters; holding the ihawu (shield) - which symbolises protection; the induku (knobkerrie) and a spear which were left by her grandfather - for looking after the home.

Ncube was nearly killed at a competition which was held in Harare by a male Imbongi. The male Imbongi tried to attack Elizabeth with a spear as she was performing, but Elizabeth overpowered the man. She attributed the overpowering of this man to the warrior spirit that guides her. She won the competition, beating the two men whom she was competing with. When Elizabeth met the man some months later and confronted him on why he had wanted to beat her, the man said (Wake wabona ngaphi umfazi otanyula inyawo pambili kwabantu!) "Were did you see a woman who opens her legs in front of people!"

In 1991 she performed in Chicago, Milwaukee, Boston, Detroit (USA), before going to Toronto (Canada) in 1992 and, later, to Holland. Despite initial serious resistance and controverse, her perseverance heralded the groundbreaking entry of a female into the predominantly male Imbongi domain.

Date

Date

Date

Irene Chigamba

IRENE Chigamba's home environment provided a good opportunity which enabled her to do well in the music industry. She performed with her family, and the public space became familiar. This also created confidence in her. When Chigamba started playing mbira she was discouraged by relatives. "They would say that I would never get married because I had ventured into a man's world. They would also try to convince my mother to try and stop me as this was going to bring bad spirits to me, but my mother stood by me," Irene also plays drums.

Irene's father Tute Chigamba who had learnt how to play the mbira from his wife Laiza (Irene's mother) although he found it difficult to acknowledge that he had learnt the instrument from his wife, taught his daughter (Irene) to play mbira.

Irene was taught by her father not only to play the mbira, but also to repair the instrument: "He took me as his daughter, not as someone who did not matter, because he saw my love for the mbira, and since I was the only girl in the family who was interested (then). He also enjoyed and loved teaching me the mbira. He also taught me to make the instrument; he can also repair the mbira." When someone is given knowledge they also want to pass it to others, and on to the younger generation, as Irene did that. She and other performers formed the National Dance Company. Irene started teaching youngsters in 1984. The group was called The Young Zimbabweans.

Irene Chigamba went on to research on the meaning of the dances that she was teaching and has been to different places researching why certain drums were being played. She wishes women could take time to learn instruments. "Generally, women's confidence has been shattered, and they need to be encouraged."

Daisy Chenjerayi

Daisy Chengerayi could not escape the family's musical talent, music was all over her. She started by performing at Ambuya Chiramba Kusaka's programmes and she would also sing at home with her mother who gave her advice. When her mother heard her sing Zai Regondo she encouraged her to record the song which became popular in the 80's. She also featured in a programme Mhuri yavaMukadota with her mother and late sister Petronella, popularly known as Chimbwido.

"When I was growing up when my mother was rehearsing it was as if she is on stage so I really liked it so after watching her rehearsal we would go behind the house and would start to do own rehersals." Said Daisy who also got encouragement from her peers at school, she also got encouragement from big people in the industry who would give her praises in public. "I enjoyed the way people used to praise us, even old people I remember Webster Shamu when he met me when there were people he would greet me and introduce me to people so it made me feel great [Webster Shamu is a well known personality in politics and music, and he is the current Zimbabwe Minister of Information.) When Daisy got married she was lucky that her husband and in-laws did not see it as a problem that she was a musician but continued to encourage and be proud of her.

However Daisy feels that women do not take music a serious business that is why men are more than women in the music industry as man take it not just as a talent but as a source of encome. She feels women take music as a hobby and pastime which has to change.

Besides the song Zai Regondo she recorded the songs; Eriya Waenda, Tibatsireyi Jehova and Usatambudzike uchiratidza vana in 1989.

Jackie Cahi

JACKIE Cahi was born in Bulawayo in 1956, but grew up in Harare. She was born at a time when the Golden Rhythm Crooners and the Cool Four were highly popular. Little did she predict that some day she would be the promoter of Cool Crooners.

Jackie never grew up in an African township, but as a musician she got familiar with a lot of township music. She became part of a group called Solidarity, just after Independence, which also comprised of Paul Brickhill, Shacky Kangwena and Washington Kavhai. The latter two went on to form the Bhundu Boys. As vocalist, she got exposed to townships, mines, and farms; subsequently the group became a success story of the 80's. Within the musical fraternity, Jackie met the Cool Crooners and eventually became their promoter. She believes the sky is the limit, for the singing quartet. Jackie produced a film documentary on the Cool Crooners – Blue Sky in 2002, which was received very well locally and internationally.

Debbie Metcalf

Debbie Metcalf has been in the music industry for decades, she followed the footsteps of earlier white women promoters who were around in the 1950'. Women who were around in the 1950's were Eileen Haddon, Monica Marsden and Barbara Tredgold, there were interested in black music and theatre and worked hard to promote them. In 1985, Debbie in partnership with two sound engineers, established, co-owned and managed a 16 / 24 track recording studio in Harare called Frontliine Studio where all major Zimbabwean groups on the charts came to record, some of them were the Bhundu Boys, Thomas Mapfumo, Oliver Mtukudzi and regional artists.

The acquisition of a stadium-capacity professional sound system saw the company serve well over a hundred major 'live' music events all over Zimbabwe and many more smaller events (corporates / club and conference centres).

By 1994, she assumed full-time management of Oliver Mtukudzi who she began working closely with after the recording of his album 'Strange Isn't It" at Frontline Studio in 1985. "I never considered becoming an artist manager and only learnt what it entailed from my early dealings with Oliver (and the Black Spirits) and Steve Dyer (with Southern Freeway) with whom I seemed to find a natural affinity from the day I met them and we effectively built our careers together. I have always enjoyed the contact with the musicians the most, bottom-up approach one could call it, but it was those relationships that kept me buoyant when the going got tough which was regularly!"

During the time she was his manager/promoter, Oliver's musical career reached higher levels. "Until January 2007, I maintained my position as Manager of both artists (Steve Dyer and Oliver Mtukudzi)."

Date

Date

Date

Music:
Age old stress relief tool

Do women know how to make economic use of their traditional music?

Music helped women to cope with their day-to-day work. For instance, when working in the fields, pounding and thrashing (maize, millet or sorghum), they sang songs in rhythm with the way they were doing the particular task and in no time they would be through. This made their work easier, and less stressful. The sound produced by the pounding sticks and thrashing was in itself musical.

Women also created stories for each age group of children, and for the various life-cycle stages. These stories were almost always accompanied by music that was composed simultaneously, to suit the mood and the story. The storyteller would involve her listeners/audience in the song as a way of making sure that they understood what she is trying to put across.

Unfortunately, in general, women musicians have not known how to make the best economic use of this rich legacy because they have not known how to rework work songs, lullabies, wedding songs and other songs traditionally associated with women for the domain of popular music.

In present day Zimbabwean society as is the case with many other countries in Africa; it is regarded as a woman's main duty to give birth and to look after the children. In many African traditions, in order to make the task of motherhood more bearable and enjoyable, women found ways to deal with the different challenges of childcare. Women composed songs to communicate with children. Lullabies were used to comfort young children, to persuade them to go to sleep, as well as to communicate with them.

While women were singing these songs to children they were being passed on to future generations, and are part of the heritage of being a Zimbabwean/African woman.

The first person to translate women's musical heritage into popular music effectively was the South African singer Miriam Makeba. She recorded the widely known Nguni lullaby 'Thula Sana Lwami' in the 1950's and it became so popular that it is now recognised as a Southern African jazz standard. She reclaimed this song on behalf of women in general.

Miriam Makeba inspired other women to also record lullabies and other children's songs. For instance, in 1994, Tendai Makura recorded Shona lullabies and other children's songs. She worked with nine children who sang with her and took part in the recording. As they sang together the lullabies and songs for children's games, Makura passed the music on to today's generations. Some of the songs on this recording are Usachema Mwana (Do not cry child), Mwana Wangu Chivata (Sleep my child), E-ru-ru-re. E-ru-ru-re (Hush-hush, my baby, don't you cry). E-ru-ru-re, is a popular Shona lullaby. When we were growing up in the township we used to sing this song while babysitting.

Some of the music women provided were during weddings. In an Nguni wedding women were in charge of welcoming the bride into her parents-in-law's home. In Ndebele (Nguni) culture the welcoming ceremony was called ukuhaya. Ukuhaya was delegated to women of high standing in their communities who were professionals in this regard. My maternal grandmother, Malandu Mateza (Mangena), who was also a storyteller, would be invited to welcome the bridegroom in ukuhaya in her home area Gwatemba (Filabusi). She was of big built but when she was involved in ukuhaya she would jump and do all that was necessary to perform ukuhaya well. Therefore she was always invited to welcome the bride into her new family. Malandu was also reputed to have been one of the best dombo (bride price negotiators between the bridegroom and the bride's family) in the community, even though negotiating for bride price was a role mostly assigned to men.

A woman rather than a man usually performs Ukuhaya in order to make another woman feel at ease in her new home and family.

'Halala halala, Hoza laye, hoza laye !' (Halala halala 'bring her, bring her (to the family) !') they would sing, mentioning the name of the bride and the bridegroom (her husband) who would be holding her as they walk into his family home. The leader of the welcoming group of women would then jump jubilantly towards the bride reciting poetry which is backed by song by the other women whom she is leading and making gestures symbolising 'welcome home' amid ululations and the waving of a cow's tail.

This is how Doric Sithole who comes from afamily of women who are involved in ukuhaya explains the ukuhaya, "Ukuhaya is a celebration which is done so as to welcome the new bride into the family. Very often other women who are her in-laws in song and in dance welcome the bride. An interesting point to note about this celebration is the fact that the lyrics of the songs are a reflection of the roles of the bride/woman in the family". She goes on to exaplain, "The main reason why women take part in this celebration and not men is because women who welcome the bride have more experience about what is expected from a woman hence it is always best to be welcomed by people who will give you advice about how to do things when one is married".

Like the Ndebele, in Shona culture the husband's relatives sang songs that showed that they were happy to have their new daughter- in-law, particularly the husband's sisters (vana-tete).

This is part of the Shona practice called "kushonongora mwenga" (to show acceptance of the bride by giving her money, and also to honour her). The songs they sang included Tauya naye muroora (We have brought the daughter in-law home). The female relatives of the husband to welcome the new bride, to her new home and family usually sang the songs. The song Tauya naye muroora was rearranged by David Chifunyise, and was given a new urban grooves feel. The other song often sung was

Muroora ndewedu (The bride is ours).

It is unfortunate that women musicians have not taken traditional music seriously as male musicians have.
In the 1960's the City Quads a township male jazz group, rearranged and recorded Nguni traditional wedding songs; Nyathel' Ugqihile, Lamlela and Dalala Khece. I wish young women musicians could do their own versions of wedding songs in their different genres; jazz, pop, urban grooves, etc. They should also perform at weddings like the Jelimusolu women ensemble in Bamako who are an indispensable act at weddings, they perform at marriage festivals and this has become a major source of income for them.

Women should be innovative and look out for opportunities in the music industry, how women can benefit from traditional music is one opportunity. Some women traditional/popular musicians have had problems taking traditional music to another level because of the rituals that the music is associated with. They sometimes feel that they are not doing the right thing, and yet male musicians have found an opportunity in popularizing traditional songs and have made a fortune. Male musicians have popularized the music to the extent that they have taken some of the music, which was sung by women traditionally. Women seem not to have the knowledge that they could also change traditional music into popular music and benefit from it just like their male counterparts. Thomas Mapfumo and Salif Keita are some of the musicians who have rearranged traditional music into pop and made it on the popular music scene. The men have done it with a clear conscience, but some female musicians would want to be apologetic about it.

The late Elizabeth Ncube did well as the first female praise poet, which was mostly a male domain. Despite having done well in this field she still had mixed feelings on the way traditional music is being presented that it was no longer the same with how it was presented in the olden days. In my interview with her in the 1990's, she said, "We held a traditional dance between rural and urban women, I realized that there was a big difference between the dances. Women in the city are no longer dancing as we did in the rural areas, its diluted, even if they are dancing isitshikitsha, its not like traditional isitshikitsha, people are now dancing fast even the clapping of hands, its now to fast. Even the Hosana if for instance I play drums with a person from the rural areas it is no longer the same, because things have changed".

She lamented, "I see that I am also changing some of the traditional music like Hosana and putting it into records. It's now mixed with guitars not that I am saying it's wrong. It depends ngokuntshintsha kwezinto, kodwa amadhlozi kajabuli (it is because things are changing but ancestral spirits are not happy) but anyway (ngokuhamba kumele kubikwe) (as time goes on we have to inform the ancestors) that we are doing whatever we are doing because of ABC".

I encourage women to enjoy the fruits of the music that was passed on to you, ancestors will be happy if the music heritage they left would benefit you, in order to be able to look after yourself and their great grandchildren. They would want you to get financial rewards from that music because it is your right and they love you.

Celebrate womanhood through music.

Date

Chiwoniso Maraire

When Chiwoniso's parents (Dumisani Maraire and Linda Nemarundwe –Maraire), encouraged their daughter to play mbira, little did they know that she would be the queen of mbira and today Chiwonsio is known in Zimbabwe and internationally as one of the best mbira players. She inspired many young musicians to be proud of the mbira instruments because of the way she mastered the instrument and expressed herself. Some young musicians mostly women did not want to associate themselves with mbira because of how it had been interpreted that it was not supposed to be played by women. Dumi Maraire Chiwoniso's father disputed that notion as he himself played the mbira because eof his great grandmother and passed on this gift to Chiwoniso.

Despite having spent the day working, when Dumisani got home he would play mbira for Chii as she was affectionately known, who would always ask her father to play mbira for her before she went to sleep. Besides mbira music being a lullaby for her, Chiwoniso learnt a lot from the way her father played mbira, as she was a great imitator. This resulted in Chiwoniso playing mbira at the age of four, as and when she would pick up the instrument in the house - until her father gave her one, her first mbira instrument. At the age of nine she was already playing on stage with her parents, brothers and sisters. At school Chiwoniso was also encouraged to sing by her choir teacher, who was very much aware of her music abilities, and gave her all the support.

Chiwoniso Maraire revolutionized mbira music by adding English lyrics and church songs. It was a natural choice for Chii. She was born in Washington State, the United States where her Zimbabwean parents were studying and teaching mbira. She wrote music for the sound track to the Zimbabwean hit film Everyone's Child. Chiwoniso won many musical awards.

Chiwoniso who passed on, on the 24th July 2013 has left a legacy!

Busi Ncube

THE 1980's saw Busi Ncube coming up with a different kind of sound, which did not really belong to a particular genre although it could be classified as Afro pop music. It was a fusion of different rhythms, and she sung mostly in Ndebele and English, she is said to sing in other four languages according to Wikipedia. Now based in Norway, Busi was a member of the group Ilanga and she made her name with a song called I want True Love, based on the tune Imi Munosara Nani Ndaenda tune. With the groups Illanga, the group recorded three albums in the 1980's and played during the Human Rights Concert - Now concert.

When Ilanga broke up she continued on her own and she is one of the few women in charge of a band, and she owned her own instruments. Her group was called Band Rain. Busi was involved in a number of projects in the music scene. With her backing band, Band Rain Busi recorded eight albums, including Malaisha and Live in Prague. The band toured Norway in 2006 and appeared at the Mela Festival. Ncube has also contributed to another Thulani project, "The Collaboration" which produced the album Hupenyu Kumusha/Life at Home released in 2006. She also plays the mbira.

During her time with Band Rain the group did well and she attributes this to the good and transparent management skills that she had, and the openness that she had with her band. She made sure that all the band members had access to the ledger books, and everyone was satisfied: "This way everyone in the group is kept in the picture, and whatever money we will have made at any show is shared accordingly." Not being transparent amongst band members has sometimes seen musical groups disbanding.

Based in Norway, Busi continues to grow in music.

Irene Gwaze

*I*rene Gwaze has groomed several young musicians to artistic fruition. Musicians have often sought the liberal guidance of Irene. The Red Fox Hotel, which her family used to own, became a hub and haven of aspiring and upcoming musicians. She hosted a number of jazz festivals, including The National Hunger Concert. Some bands she promoted included; The Other Four, Summer Breeze, Cool Crooners, Ernest Tanga wekwa Sando, Africa Revenge, Dumi Ngulube & Amagents, Patricia Matongo and Colour Blu, which she used to manage. She often offered free accommodation to particular groups, and rehearsing space for upcoming musicians.

Irene's love for Afro-jazz is a result of growing up in Bulawayo's Makokoba Township, where the unique music was flourishing. She is an exceptional female music promoter, who has contributed greatly towards to the maturity of young jazz artists.

Taruwona Mushore

Failing to put in place structures that benefit women musicians and women in general in public space has been a disadvantage in the development of women across the board as it affects women performers and audience members. Women, in general, are misrepresented in music. The purpose of music in the society, as a vehicle for change and tool for communication, is not realized, this end up benefiting men, who set these structures.

According to one woman musician Taruwona Mushore, because of the defined structures in public sphere women musicians end up acquiring a certain persona or faking a certain persona in order for them to fit, be accepted, or to be able to survive. She changed her persona in order to survive in public space.

"I think I managed to get confidence, but I think to the detriment of my performance, because here is what I was doing: I would go and give my soul and then, immediately, I would become another image. I would become sort of a hardened person where if anyone wanted to approach me in any way I would immediately cut them and defend myself, but that's not the way I feel. As a performer I feel that you portray your performances. You become what you are performing, but I don't think you should separate. You shouldn't be another person. I don't think you have to recondition yourself to do something else. I feel it's a reflection of me, that's how it should be. So, immediately I was assuming another persona which was not what I wanted to be, the hardened woman who is going to be more liberated than liberated" Said Taruwona who rose to fame with her song I met Dambudziko in 1992, which became an instant hit.

Taruwona's wish is to create a friendly venue which will accommodate women and children.

Date

Date

Date

Women Musicians and Access to economic power –

Women musicians need access to economic power

L imited access to economic power has made it difficult for women to function in the music sphere as musicians, bandleaders, managers, promoters and producers. As a result, women end up as backing vocalists and dancers, at the mercy of their male counterparts and bosses.

To be a bandleader, manager, promoter or producer needs financial back up, which women generally do not have. As a result, men end up dominating the positions of power in the music industry. Men are the ones who determine what happens in the music industry because they finance the music projects. They have had easy access to finance, mostly because of how the structures of the society favour men. Money is part of men's vocabulary and it is made easy by the associations that men have control over. They meet in places where the "who-is-who" of the society socializes. Because of these connections, it is easy for men to access bank loans or be told where they can get financial assistance.

Women's lack of access to economic power in the music business is a result of many factors, such as: the way women view or perceive money, and the way the family is structured (to disempower women). Families do not instil a sense of ownership and belonging as girls grow up. Issues such as inheritance are also discriminatory to women as a daughter, and as a wife. Lack of access to economic power has seen women taking up any job that will be available in the music industry. They usually start as backing vocalists or dancers and may not progress beyond that.

While women contribute to the family in so many ways as daughters and as wives, they are usually at the receiving end. This is because they are "owned" as daughters, and as wives. Whatever they bring to the family becomes family property, just like they themselves are seen as family property. For centuries economic power has been associated with authority. This is why men cannot readily let it go into the hands of women. The way money has been presented to women is as if it is associated with some 'evil' but, with men, it is associated with glory and status. Although it is said that "money is the root of all evil", the opposite is very true; More money, appropriately used, is the root of happiness, stability, status and power. Women should understand that, and not be ashamed of having money – even in abundance.

There are few women who have done relatively well in their musical careers. They have been able to generate sizeable incomes for themselves, thereby benefiting economically from music. These are the women who have had to work very hard, doing more than one thing in the music and the arts industry. However, this is only a very small proportion of women in music today. They have read into the whole spectrum of the music terrain in order to understand its other components, which are not just music performance.

Women bandleaders benefit more, as they are in control of their finances. (It is however advisable to have a manager, so as not to compromise their creativity.) Women who team up with their husbands may, or may not, benefit that much – depending on the dynamics between the couple. Of course, every active and performing musician is probably earning an income, but very few women have made significant financial gains in the music industry. Right now, women benefit much less economically, from music, than most men do. This is due to the mere fact that the local music industry is primarily in male hands.

Women have to deal with a number of layers in the society in order for them to understand what is going on out there. This results in a few women as managers and promoters.
In the past, leaders of all-female groups also doubled as managers. Victoria Chingate led and managed the Gay Gaieties, an all-female group formed in 1954. Around the same time Sylvia Sondo also led and managed the all-female group, The Yellow Blues.

The 1950's also saw women promoters, such as Eileen Haddon, Barbara Tredgold and Monica Marsden, who were interested in the black music and theatre. They worked hard to promote township music and theatre.

Some of the women who have taken up Music Promotion are Irene Gwaze, Jackie Cahi, Rhoda Mandaza, Penny Yon, Barbara Chikosi, Priscilla Sithole and Tsungi Zvobgo.

Irene Gwaze has groomed several young musicians to artistic fruition. The budding township musicians have often sought the liberal guidance of Irene.

Jackie Cahi met the Cool Crooners and eventually became their promoter, she went on to produce a film documentary on the Cool Crooners.

Rhoda Mandaza has been involved a number of music projects as a promoter, music producer and also producing the videos.

Tsungi Zvobgo has been managing Victor Kunonga and Chiwoniso Maraire among other musician.

While she was administrator and later Director at Amakhosi, Priscilla Sithole promoted women musicians to realize their goal, one of the groups that she promoted is Amakhosikazi awomen's group.

Barbara Chikosi the Managing Director of Red Rose Entertainment is a promoter who has promoted a number of the artists in the country.

Penny Yon has contributed to Township Music as both performer and promoter. Penny was involved with Jazz festivals during 1996 – 1999. She did not stop at organising festivals but also marketed jazz musicians, acting as their agent, since she worked for a tourism company. Her desktop publishing expertise facilitated dissemination and publicity of festival material. She would do posters, newspaper ads, flyers and complementary tickets. At times she used her phone, fax and email for business contacts.

The nature of the music industry can erode one's income if one does not keep adding on or generating money from the music venture, or from other sources. Some of the musicians who have made it have been able to get financial support from other sources, besides music. They may have a side job to subsidize their music endeavors. Laura Bezuidenhout, is one musician who has subsidized her musical career with a side job: "It takes a very "big" heart to keep going. I, on the other hand, do not have such a big heart, but am rather a coward, choosing to fall back on other skills from time to time to recuperate financially and obtain the necessary resources. I'm lucky in that I have other skills and capabilities that allow me to earn an income outside of the music industry. I have used this over the years to procure the necessary resources to be able to remain independent". She continues, "It has meant "dropping out" of "musical circulation" for years at a time, working and saving for whatever the necessities are: keyboards, amplifiers & peripherals, a car, etc. I doubt that I would have managed in any other way, given the poverty, abuse and disrespect encountered in the music industry. That is why I have determined to remain independent, even at the risk of being musically dormant for long periods of time".

Being able to get funds outside the music realm has made it possible for some female musicians to sustain their musical careers, as music alone does not pay that much. This is made worse by the fact that women fall at the bottom end of the ladder in the hierarchy of the music industry, mostly as backing vocalists. They do not understand the music business, and are exploited for their ignorance. Instrumentalists seem to be paid more than backing vocalists and dancing girls. This means that there are not many women who become financially viable in music, as there are not many female instrumentalists, even bandleaders. All this affects women musicians' ability to function in the music business. They lack resources, which results in the lack of ownership. In the end they cannot fully own their product, just as they have not been able to own most things in their lives. Taruwona Mushore who made a name for herself in the mid 1990's with her classical "I met Dambudziko", managed to own her musical products by subsidizing her music projects with her other job. In an interview that I had with her in 1995, she said, "I am fortunate enough to have another occupation because I would be disillusioned, if solely relied on music. It's something that I'm very interested in doing."

Depending on doing other jobs for financial support has seen women musicians disappearing for sometime from the music scene, and then coming back when they have enough funds to run their musical projects. Jane Chenjerayi's first love is music. She started music at an early age and, had she had it her way, she would just be in music and not any other place. But unfortunately, like some of her colleagues, she disappears from the music scene in order to work so that she can be able to survive. In the 1970's, she used to combine music and her other job, until she became a full time musician. When she realized that the music business was going down, she went back to work outside music. Recently, Jane Chenjerayi was working in South Africa to raise money for her musical projects.

However, a few women musicians have had access to economic power in the music business. This is because there are few women who can control the means of production in the music industry, and across the board. Not many women own musical instruments, or the venues were music is played. There are also not many women in the recording industry, or as bandleaders. This is all because; the women's financial base is weak.

Generally, in the workplace, women are not well paid (historically). This makes it difficult for them to support other women in the entertainment industry, like by attending their shows, as they would want to spread the little they have on 'important family activities'. There is a mentality that women should earn less than men for the same kind of job. This is a mentality that the society uses even when paying women musicians.

Lack of access to economic power for women musicians is carried on from how the society operates – that women are worth less. Women in Zimbabwe had to fight their male counterparts for equal pay across the board, and women in the music business are no exception.
Women, as you continue multi-tasking your way up the music ladder, do it in such a way that you celebrate life and womanhood.

Date

Tendai Ziyambe

TENDAI Ziyambe's understanding of music education saw her resigning from her sales lady paying job and enrolled with the Zimbabwe College of Music (Ethnomusicology Dept.) Despite being the only woman in the class, she did not feel out of place, because she had found what she wanted to do. The programme was sponsored which made it easy for her as she did not have any source of income and she had just had a baby. "We didn't pay anything, we only brought books. The diploma involved learning different cultures, theory and physical instruments but the sad part is that I was the only woman and with about ten guys, and last two years before they were only two women for the diploma." Zimbabwe College of Music is one institution which has tried to support women in music education.

Tendai attributes the lack of female students to the way society view women musicians, when she told her father that she wanted to enroll as a music student at the college, he was not happy and she said that this is the way society feels.

"I think like the way my father used to think that if you are in music you are seen like someone who is loose having a lot of man and living an immoral life. But it's like work like any other work, music is in me and I can't do without music."

After the diploma Tendai did research in traditional musical instruments found in Zimbabwe. "It was quite interesting because I didn't know that Zimbabwe had so many instruments some which I had never seen before."

Tendai and other women started a group called Tonderai Women's Perfomers, which among other things taught and encouraged women to play instruments.

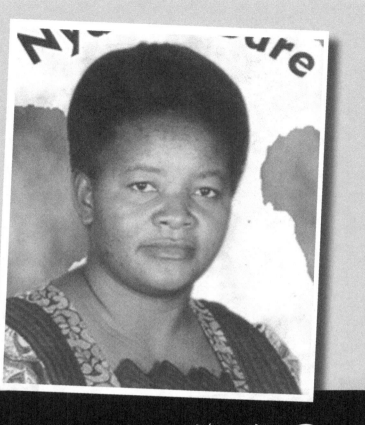

Nyasha Bare

NYASHA Bare's love of music saw her being the first student to be enrolled at the The Zimbabwe College of Music (Ethnomusicology of Zimbabwe). "I had interest in music from a very young age up to when I started my primary education. I used to participate in school choirs and traditional dance groups and when I went to secondary school I was a choir leader for Sunday school and I also used to conduct a school choir at boarding school. After my secondary education I was a temporary choir mistress for six years. My choir used to come out number one or two. So my interests and skills developed and then one day I saw an advert in the paper for Ethnomusicology, there were inviting applicants for music students. I then applied and I was the first student to be recruited at the Ethnomusicology College."

Nyasha Bare, is now a teacher at Avondale Primary School. "People didn't understand what I would do in life with such a course. Some thought a person who did such a course would join a band, not knowing that it's just like any other course, whereby you have practical and oral lessons and also sit for exams. Music is just like any other subject. So people used to look down upon what I was doing (the course). They didn't see it as a decent profession, especially for women." She said in an interview.

Nyasha's family did not understand about music education, and they had to see her conduct lessons, in order to believe and understand what she was doing. It was a surprise for Nyasha's family when she started working. They did not really understand how she did it. Society has to be educated on formal music education, and also be shown that it can be part of mainstream education.

Nomsa Ncube

NOMSA Ncube made her mark as one of the few women to play drums. She enrolled at Amakhosi in 1983 and was involved in acting. When Amakhosi was offering lessons on drum playing she took the opportunity. Although it was difficult at first, as the whole body would be sore after playing the drums, she persevered and she mastered the skill.

"It's really difficult but if you understand it and you have interest it's not all that hard, you should just follow what they will be doing and especially if you have interest it won't be that difficult."

While women have made reasonable strides in playing instruments very few women have ventured into learning how to play drums.

Prudence Katomeni-Mbofana

PRUDENCE was born long after female giants, Lina Mattaka, Evelyn Juba, Dorothy Masuka and Faith Dauti. Nevertheless, she has created a musical niche for herself as a seasoned Township/Jazz Musician. "I just go into a natural high, and I am just transferred into a different world," she narrates.

Prudence started off by imitating Makeba and Masuka, before composing and rearranging her own songs. Today she is a celebrated jazz artist in her own right.

Born in Harare in 1977, to a family of musicians; Prudence admired her aunts who sang in the church choir. At school she joined drama and experienced Dub Poets by Albert Nyathi. She later worked with Thando Maclaren, who was involved in theatre and drama productions.

Prudence joined the group called Vice, where she had the first experience as jazz singer. She was the youngest in the group, with most members over the age of thirty. After three years with Vice, she went solo and performed at different functions as well as corporate receptions.

When Sam Mataure conceived the idea a "Moving Jazz Café", Prudence banded together with Jazz Invitation, comprising of Kelly·Rusike, Ritchie Lopez and Filbert Marova. The group produced an Afro-Jazz album: Rehearsal Room, containg a 50's hit; "Ndafunafuna", a composition of Sonny Sondo. Her voice is enriching throughout the album.

Prudence teams up with top musicians such as The Cool Crooners, who have requested her to feature on their recording tracks. She has also often staged alongside Oliver Mtukudzi and Tanga wekwa Sando.

Prudence has just released a CD Titled Prudence, the album is diverse and a great listen. With this work, the songstress asserts her own unique and strong musical identity.

Date

Date

Date

Zimbabwe Women and Music Education

WOMEN'S careers are mostly determined by how they have been allowed to dream as they grow. There are limits to how far a woman can go regards dreaming which leads to her career choices. Patriarchy controls women's minds by limiting women's aspirations by the way they control their ability to dream.

Access to education which is a stepping stone to dreaming big can be limited to women depending on whether the resources available can accommodate them. Formal education is often made available to the boy child more than the girl child. Further, boys are allowed to experiment and if they fail, they are still encouraged and given support.

Girls are generally not supposed to fail, therefore women become afraid to try out new things including getting access to knowledge and skills. She might not go to school depending on the family's resources, which usually favours the boy child to have formal education, and she can be deprived of education.

In some families not only does a girl fail to go to school but she also has to look after her siblings while the parents are working to get financial support for the family. In case she goes to school, the way the girl child is raised at home makes her look not so intelligent.

The boy has more time for homework than the girl, as she will get home and work; cook, clean the house and other staff. In the meantime the boy child has plenty time to understand general knowledge and when they are in class the boy child has all the confidence and in most cases the girl is not very sure of what she says, her confidence is shattered, killing her voice.

Most girls in school trail behind boys. Joyce Banda now the president of Malawi tried to correct this situation by having a school just for girls. In an interview that I had with Joyce Banda in 1999 she said, that girls' only schools function much better than those which are mixed boys and girls because the girls only school brings out some strong girls who will be like 'men' in them.

Some girls feel a girls-only school can make it difficult for them to interact with men in future. Muriel Rosin, who was the only Federal MP, during the Federation of Rhodesia and Nyasaland shared the same sentiment.

When I went to school in the 1960's and 1970's, there were subjects designed for girls and boys. Girls were supposed to do domestic science subjects and boys carpentry and other 'male' subjects. Domestic science subjects involved mostly, cookery and sewing. The school education did not allow the girl child to be adventurous.

Although one would expect that with the domestic science knowledge that the girl child had, it would make it easy for her to get into one of the most lucrative careers like the hotel industry but no, this has been a male domain for a long time until recently. Although basically all the work that is performed in a hotel is the same with what women do in their homes, they could not be part of the hotel industry because it is in a public space and would allow women to have economic access.

The education system has continued into boxing the girl child into domestication. It has been proven that most girls do not take up science and technology subjects, but are inclined more to social sciences, which again makes it possible for them to be caregivers.

The issue of subject choice can also be based or determined by how much personal time women have to invest in time demanding subjects, which will lead to the same working environment in future.

When girls finish school their career choices are based on the subjects they will have done and what is accepted by the society. Most women have been exposed to teaching or nursing, secretarial or social science related courses which are to a large extent associated with care giving.

However, it is through teaching in schools that some women are exposed to music as a career that they can teach in schools.

Teaching music in schools is to some extent looked at as more respectable than performing on stage. But it is sometimes the process that one has to go through in order for them to become a qualified music teacher that ends up with a woman clashing with society. Since women teachers discover this career after they would have married and had children it becomes a problem as they are expected to spend a lot of time on the course. The course teaches amongst other subjects, music theory, instruments, research and this can be time demanding.

Most women, whom I taught at the Zimbabwe College of Music between 1991 and 2005, had problems balancing between looking after their homes and the course. Most of the women were teachers based outside Harare and had to relocate to the capital, which meant that they had to leave their children at their homes and come to Harare to look for a smaller place that they could afford to pay, because their salaries were cut and were getting three quarters of their pay.

Because of the problems they faced they ended up dropping out of the course. In a class where there was around 25 percent women and 75 percent men, a ratio of 1:4, less than a quarter of women would continue with the programme. As time went on the intake improved and there was a 50:50 representation of women and men in class.

Most women who have come to understand the broad spectrum of music have been able to do so mostly because of the families they come from or their environment.

Music is more often than not known from the performance point of view, little knowledge has been passed to society about how broad the music profession and industry is. Just like any other profession, music has to create a feeder system, which means that it has to start from Grade One in primary school up to secondary level and then to tertiary level.

With music education one can go as far as Masters Degree and PhD, specialising in particular and specific fields, for instance, Composition, Ethnomusicology, Musicology, Music Technology, Performance and Psychology of Music. Unfortunately music education has not been taken seriously; it is taken more as an extramural activity.

Rumbidzai Chipendo, chairperson of Zimbabwe Music Educators is worried about how schools need music for all the entertainment that happens at the schools but, they do not give the children the chance to learn music just like any other subject.
Although music is taught at some schools, there are no examinations set to evaluate progress.

Music is the umbrella of society. It is through music that we understand most of the aspects of our culture. The power of music is underestimated and yet if it is taken seriously, society can transmit knowledge much easier through music than some of the channels they try to use to get education. In the olden days music was used to teach and it made it easy for one to understand the knowledge that was being passed on to them, music made it lighter and more understandable. With the complexity surrounding music today, the understanding of music education has been accessed by a few and mostly men.

I came to understand music education through my parents who recognised my music talent at an early age. They encouraged me to perform and to take a music course at the College of Music, way back in the 1970's, but I did not.

Most people understand music just as performance and yet it is just like any other industry and it needs promoters, managers, sound engineers and venue owners among others. Again because the information of what makes music being not easily available, women spend more time in performance in order to be in music.

If a woman like the late Elizabeth Taderera, popularly known as Katarina, had been educated on how broad music is, she could have probably taken her dances to another level. Teaching how to dance, like Jonny Clegg who is making money by just teaching the world how to dance the Zulu contemporary dance.

I applaud women like Prudence Katomeni-Mbofana who took time off from their busy performing schedules to take up a degree in music. This is a long-term investment which will help her to talk and understand music from a well-informed position at festivals and conferences. It is not easy to take time off from performance, or from any other busy schedule in order to study music, but it is a rewarding experience.

Women it is through music education that you can understand how society functions and you can use music to protest against unfair treatment, in marriage, in the society and music can help you to celebrate life and womanhood.

Date

Benita Tarupiwa

Benita Tarupiwa a mbira player, has played with different groups since 1987 to 1996 when she formed her group Negombwe Mbira group. In 1997 she went to Switzerland by herself and recorded her first CD titled Ndotamba Ndega. In 1998 Benita toured Europe together with her group -Negombwe Mbira Group, on this tour together with her group recorded her second CD 'Shirikadzi' which is a live-recording of one of the concerts.

Benita started playing mbira when she was four years old. She would go to biras (night virgils) being carried on the back by her mother as she was one of the mbira players in the group. The group was known as a group as group with one mbira which plays itself, as the person who was playing it was not seen, she would be covered in the mbira deze (cover for mbira) and she was Benita at four. Tarupiwa remembers having a dream being taught how to play the instrument by her grandfather (great uncle), she was later to meet her grandfather through the instrument that he played when he was still alive which is a mbira that she later played.

She has been to many countries playing the mbira instrument sometimes performing and sometimes teaching how to play. She has been to Canada, Switzerland, Netherlands to name a few.

As from 2002 Benita has slowed down as a result of a number of factors the major one was the loss of her instruments which were sold by her brother, "My brother took advantage of my being a woman and thought he could do whatever he wanted with my instruments while I was travelling abroad giving lectures and performing, this has seriously affected my work."

Recently she performed for a children's home to raise funds, and she is slowly making a full come back into music performance.

Naome Makwenda

NAOME Makwenda was born into a family which is immersed in music. From a tender age she sang with her mother, Joyce Jenje-Makwenda,

During her pre-school days, she and her friends had a singing group. A teacher at the pre-school commented: "It would be sad if you just let that talent go to waste". Joyce mentored her in voice perfection but, after noticing her keen interest in music, also went on to recruit a personal mbira tutor for Naome and the family.

She became a professional artist at age 11, after featuring in "Senzeni Na Video" – a 1995 all-time hit music video for a song composed by Albert Nyathi, initially sung by Prudence Katomene-Mbofana. With only a day to practise, and help from her mother, Joyce, Naome's voice and body language output were so polished that the video elevated her to great heights in the arts. Consequently, she went on to do tours and other performances around Zimbabwe with: Albert and Imbongi; Ihawu LeSizwe; the Soul Brothers, and others - mostly for charitable causes – with, amongst others, UN-ESCO and other organisations.

Naome also did modelling for print and electronic media, and fashion houses before venturing into film acting for television from 1996.

Naome is currently living in the UK, still plays the mbira, and is also learning to play the guitar. Although not into music full time, she still sessions with some bands, including a rock group.

Patricia Matongo

or a long time the one solo guitarists scene was dominated by man, there were called omasiganda or gwenyambira or as one man band guitarists. Patricia came onto the music scene and made her mark as one of the few women solo guitarists – a one woman band guitarist. Patricia carved her space in this once very male dominated genre/style. Her music is between Jiti and some country style influence. The way she blends her guitar playing and her voice is mesmerizing. She got interested in Jiti music because it was her mother's favourite music.

From an early age Patricia was fascinated by music and in 1998, she enrolled at the Zimbabwe College of Music; Saturday Pop Workshops and was lucky that her tutor was the renowned guitarist in Zimbabwe – the late Andrew Chakanyuka. It took her a year to become an accomplished guitarist/musician and in 1999 she came up with an album.

Her debut album in 1999, Musarovane was received very well by a wide section of people as the title track addresses issues to do with domestic violence. In this song she is discouraging men to beat up their wives. Musarovane sold more than 1000 copies. Another song on the album; Wakanga Uripo rechead number one on Radio's top 10 in April 2000.

Patricia is now based in South Africa were she has been working with artists and she continues with her music.

Laina Gumboreshumba

Laina Gumboreshumba, a mbira player/teacher was also encouraged by her father Gwanzura Gumboreshumba to play mbira. Gwanzura Gumboreshumba recorded a mbira video with Andrew Tracy in 1975. Laina, like Irene Chigamba and Chiwoniso Maraire, performed with her father at biras and concerts. She has taken mbira music to another level, as she is doing a PhD at the Rhodes University in Ethnomusicology.

Her family gave her both moral and financial support. Gumboreshumba was also encouraged by her schoolteacher to join the school choir, which helped nurture her talent. "I was in grade 6, the school choir was having one of their practice sessions. I was playing with my friend under a Musasa tree. The choirmaster, Mr Mhishi, happened to pass by. He picked me up and said to me, "Go and join the choir". I was shocked that how could he ask me to join the choir at this point in time when the choir had been practicing for over 2 months. Would I be able to catch up with the others at all! At the same time I was so excited to join the school choir".

She grew up dancing to mbira music at mapira (ancestral night vigils) and other traditional ceremonies, which her father used to hold at their home. Attending traditional ceremonies with her father made her to fall in love with mbira music at a very tender age. Her father was a gwenyambira (virtuoso mbira player) and she used to gaze, in admiration, when he played mbira.

"I also admired his philosophy about life, his wit and humour. He inspired me in so many ways, through his intriguing stories about his own experiences in life, and always emphasised that, as long as one is determined to succeed, nothing is impossible." Her father was her idol. He also taught Stella Chiweshe to play mbira.

Date

Date

Date

Amakhosikazi

A makhosikazi - an all-female band - was founded by Priscilla Sithole who natured the group. Besides instrument playing, singing and dancing, the women also do sound engineering, stage designing, and other more technical aspects of music.

The group benefited from the different cultures of its thirteen members, two of them from outside Zimbabwe: Thembi Ngwabi - dancer, actress and musician - also featured in a number of productions; Edith Katiji - lead singer and dancer - formerly lead singer with Mabhiza, also played a supporting role in 'Sinjalo' - a television sit-com; Fatima Katiji - whose career started in church before entering mainstream arts industry through Amakhosi; Patience Nxumalo - keyboards; Thubelihle 'Thuba' Mpofu; Virgnia Ncube - dancer and backing vocalist - trained with Amakhosi Theatre's Children Programme and has worked with several music groups; Simangaliso 'Manyox' Nyoni - acoustic guitar - has also recorded an album, 'Ukuthandana'; Proper 'Professor' Maphosa - Bongo drum - also a member of Usiko Lwabokhokho, a traditional group that plays mostly 'Amabhiza', a Kalanga form of dance; Precious Sibanda - who started off as backing singer for Lwazi Tshabangu's group; Rea Moyo - drums, percussion, mbira - a multi-talented artist, who also plays traditional instruments; Asha Salim Mshana (originally from Tanzania) - with a Diploma in performance (Performing) Arts from Bagamoyo College of Arts and a Diploma in directing from Sweden; Clemantina Zimba (originally from Mozambique) - marimba, lead vocals; Priscilla Sithole - Artistic Director - one of the few widely-experienced arts managers, having been involved in arts projects in and outside Zimbabwe. .

Through Priscilla Sithole's guidance the group rose to stardom and gave birth to one of the celebrated female guitarist Edith weUtonga. Besides the launch of the Zimbabwe International Film Festival (ZIFF), Amakhosikazi participated in numerous concerts and the group made waves in the music industry.

Julia Chigamba

ancing is part of her life and when she is dancing she goes into a world that even cameras sometimes fail to capture her as she goes into full motion. "It was when I got to the US, that I was given the title – dancer, but for me it is just part of my life" Said Julia Chigamba in an interview I had with her at the Cultural Centre she built in Hatfield, Harare recently.

She surprised many when she performed her dances when she was only left with two weeks to deliver her baby, but to her this is part of her life. One day when she had a show with her group in Oakland people commented that when she was dancing all they could see were ancestral spirits on the stage. Julia Tsitsi Chigamba's background provided her with the dancing talent that she is today sharing with the world. Her parents Tute and Laiza Chigamba were mbira players of note and her mother was a traditional dancer and musician. Her sister Irene had also paved the way for her when she was a member of the National Dance Company of Zimbabwe and founder Young Zimbabweans of Young Zimbabweans, which became Mhembero Dance Troupe and Julia became part of it. Besides being a dancer Julia Chigamba is also a singer and instrumentalist.

She is sharing her dancing skills in the USA mostly in Oakland where she has been since 1999 and founded the Chinyakare Dance Ensemble and Tawanda MuChinyakare in 2000

Julia is teaching the young and old Zimbabwe dances from Mbende, Jerusarema and Sitshikit-sha. She has even been invited to teach her traditional dance, singing and instrument playing to churches.

In their advert in 2010 ZIMFEST wrote – 'Tawanda MuChinyakare is a bridge between cultures, tribes, elders, youth and ancestors that seeks to introduce new cultural perspectives, strengthen positive aspects of heritage and expand cultural imagination. Julia's classes provide an opportunity for students to learn and experience traditional African dance and rhythms and to learn about the culture, the language and the vocal traditions of the Shona Tribes of Zimbabwe.'

Olivia Charamba

*P*opularly known as Mai Charamba by her fans, Olivia Charamba has made an impact in the Gospel Music scene. When she decided to add her voice onto the Gospel scene it was electrifying and refreshing taking Gospel music to another level.

Her musical career started when she was young singing in the church choir, were she was among the leading vocalists and she had a strong, powerful voice. She grew up in a family which were members of the Salvation Army and music became part of her, but little did she know that one day her voice was going to be heard and wow people internationally.

When Olivia Charamba left her traditional church Salvation Army to join the Apostolic Faith Mission, she was to meet her future husband Pastor Charles Charamba who would initiate her into a is a celebrated female singer; a woman of outstanding talent call her Gospel Diva if you want. She started off singing vocals in her new found church, it is when Baba Charamba as he affectionately calls him realized that she had an unusually great voice. The two have been described as pure magic. When in 2000 Charles Charamba wrote Olivia, her first album titled Amen, it became an instant and it did not give her a chance to be a novice in music she was immediately thrown into the deep end of well established musicians in the country.

Her albums to follow Amen were Daily Bread and Gospel also became instant hits and they received overwhelming support and she attributes the success of all her albums to her husband who pays attention to detail from the rehearsal room, to the studio making sure that all the instruments are talking to the voice.

Her multitasking skills have made it possible for her to juggle between being a mother of five and her hectic performing schedule although it becomes difficult when she has to travel far from the kids.

Together with her husband she has been appointed Road Safety Ambassadors by the Zimbabwe Traffic Safety Council. She is also a pastor although for now she is practicing as one.

Sister Flame

A versatile musician, Fortunate Matenga popularly known as Sister Flame is one performer whose music is difficult to classify, her music is between reggae, rock music, house music and Blues. She has performed with several bands; Imbongi (Albert Nyathi), Andy Brown. She was the lead vocalist for most of the songs on the album produced by Andy Brown and Kieth Ferguson. The project launched her as a solo artist. In 2003 she was part of an all female group which was called Ruvhuvhuto Sisters with Ivy Kombo, Jackie Madondo and Plaxedes Hwenyika. Fortunate has two albums on her sleeve; The Road and The Flame of House, she is working on her the third album. Her two albums were received very well by her followers and did well on the market.

Fortunate started her musical career at Amakhosi, just like most young people of her time who grew up in Bulawayo. It is while she was performing at Amakhosi that Albert Nyathi saw her and brought her to Harare. "When Albert Nyathi saw me perform he wanted me to be in his group Imbongi, I asked him to talk to my parents which he did. My parents were very supportive of my career, they gave me their blessings and I joined Imbongi and moved to Harare." She explained. Since then she has not looked back she takes music seriously and it is her life and she has come to understand the complicated terrain of music in its all facets; the venues, the performance side, the recording of music and music education. She also has a lot of support from her husband who is also into arts- a filmmaker.

However Fortunate Matenga wishes if there would be venues to suit the needs of women as most of the present venues are not friendly to women.

Date

Date

Date

Patience Musa

Born in 1979, Patience Musa started singing in 1999 while she was doing her A'levels at CCOSA college. She strated by doing backing vocals for different artists such as Taso, Gospel trumpet, Fungai Malianga and Mateo Kaunda. While working with Mateo, Patience also got the opportunity to write her own song and have it compiled on Mateo Kaundas album- Asambe Africa.

Besides her Music Patience was also passionate about encouraging young people to read, as she volunteered at a local organisation Zimbabwe Book Development council where she was the youth co-ordinator for the Youth forum. This led to her participating in a Swedish Youth exchange programme and her joining Forum Syd as a working member.

Patience released her first album in 2003 - With love, this project had the popular song Zvirinaani and was released through Ruffcuts promotions who were also working with Mateo at the time. In this song Patience is saying she is better off for her to be alone than to have a man who will give her problems.

In that same year Patience was nominated for a Tsama award for 'Best jazz artist', which was taken home by Mbare Trio. In 2006 Patience went on to release her next project entitled 'Patience' this time she assigned Gramma to distribute. This project introduced listeners to a mature Patience, with tracks like 'Crossroad' (Co- written with Chirikure Chirikure), Rufaro and the popular rock song What about. In 2010 after a well deserved break Patience released the c.d 'Patience Musa'.

Patience Musa has shared the stage with big names some of them, like the late Brenda Fassi, Oliver Mtukudzi, Andy Brown,Busi Ncube, Jimmy Dhludhlu, Dorothy Masuka, Hugh Masekela, Lira,Sibongile Khumalo. She is currently on her fourth album.

Patience Musa is now a producer/presenter with Zii FM.

Duduzile (Dudu) Tracy Manhenga

Duduzile "Dudu" Tracy Manhenga's mother played keyboards, whilst the grandfather played the saxophone. Born in Bulawayo in 1981, she grew up listening to music by Thembi Mtshali - a South African musician; Dorothy Masuka, and Ava Rodgers - who made inroads for her early initiation into Township Music.

At age 16 she sang with her teacher on Prize-giving days. At 17 she joined the Gospel Arch, after which she left for Siyeza, where she was a lead singer, often performing versions of Thembi Mtshali or Miriam Makeba's music.

Eager to advance her music career, she enrolled at the Zimbabwe College of Music in Harare. She then teamed up with Dumi and Amagents, led by the late Dumisani Ngulube, then a lecturer at the College. She used to split her time between performing music and college work.

Manhenga left Amagents to form a youthful group, Color Blu, and since she has recorded 4 albums. Dudu gets support from her husband who is the drummer for the group and she finds it an advantage to have a husband who is a musician as she is. Her husband is the drummer for the group she leads; Colour Blue. She explains how it is a benefit working with her husband, "I think it's much better to have someone in the industry if you come home at 2am and he will understand when you wake up at 12 in the afternoon and you still haven't cooked and will say she was working last night. Whilst if you were married to a bank teller who works from 8am to 5pm,and then at 8pm you are bathing telling him you are going out for a show, so it's easier to have a partner who is an artist who will understand the procedure that an artist has to go through"

Kudzai Sevenzo

KUDZAI Sevenzo knew what she wanted to do at a very tender age, she started singing at crèche, as soon as she left school Kudzai, joined Mhepo when she was 19. "That was my first experience with Jazz, with Live Jazz music, I always listened to Jazz Music as a child up-to today." The Afro Jazz group Mhepo natured Kudzai's talent, they would give her a chance to perform her own compositions, "I had 2 songs, they would put the music to it and I would put the lines and I was so excited, so I think that experience really molded me see one of the types of music that I would really love to do." The group would protect her in the clubs. "They would really look out for me in the clubs, when old men, where trying to hit on me.

Kudzai is not happy with the way a female musician is viewed in some of these venues. "Sometimes you need to make a statement that I'm here because of me. I find that with a female musician you always need to remind people that I'm not here to do a strip tease on stage, I'm here to sing music, fine you want to see me as that, that's your problem. I'm here to sing music, you always need to sort of draw those boundaries that this is who I am and this is where I stand but as a guy you never have to."

Kudzai was to make her big break when she represented Zimbabwe at Project Fame in 2004, although she did not make it to the end she was grateful with the experience she got. At Project Fame she got to meet big artists and one of them was Judith Sepuma. She has recorded her music and some of the CD's are; Kudzai , *Child of Africa* and *On a Day Like This.*

Nomsa Mhlanga

NOMSA Mhlanga, a young woman musician made her debut on Women's Day on the 8th August 2008. Her father, Louis Mhlanga played the guitar, accompanied her. She started her musical career when she was only four years old. Her first musical project was with her father Louis Mhlanga, when they worked on a project with abused children for the South African Broadcasting Corporation SABC, for which Nomsa composed the theme song.

At sixteen she took part in the CD/Album Women's Voices of Zimbabwe which was rearranged and produced by her father Louis Mhlanga and Joyce Jenje Makwenda, which was went by the title Four Daughters. She was the youngest of the Four Daughters and she recorded; ('Zwe Kumusha', 'Munosari Nani' and 'Nhingirikiri'), the two were originally by her grandmother (great aunt), her father's aunt Sarah Mabhokela. With music embedded deep in the family genes – she is set to reach high levels in music.

Date

Date

Date

Women Musicians and Instrument Playing

Women musicians have not made notable achievements as regards playing instruments in the music industry. It seems men dominate the playing of instruments. Lack of personal time, lack of education, lack of resources and lack of encouragement has greatly contributed to women not playing instruments. Mastering a particular instrument needs time to study it and rehearsing almost everyday. Women need to be taught how to play the instrument. It is sometimes not easy for women to get someone who is willing to teach them how. Lack of resources – instruments, venues where they can rehearse has been another stumbling block for women as regards learning an instrument. Women are not encouraged to play musical instruments as this is seen as a preserve for men.

Women have limited personal time. Their family and society determine their personal time. The unfair division of labour as girls are growing up, and when they get married, means that they do not have much time to spend on developing themselves and their talents. The demands of a musical career and the demands of marriage, (as expected by the husband and the society at large) clash.

Through determination and hard work, women musicians have been able to learn, play and be experts on certain instruments. Lina Mattaka, an early township jazz musician in the 1930's played the organ, which was very unusual.

Shuvai Wutaunashe, a gospel musician, plays the guitar. She is also a producer she encourages women not to just be singers, but also to learn to play instruments. "It takes effort, and a woman has to be able to divide her time. I am a married woman, I am a wife and I have two children. There are things I take seriously and am fortunate that my family supports me. But a woman in my position needs to have time to devote to an instrument. It just doesn't happen. You would need to spend lots of time. You can make time. Create it, because if you really love an instrument, there are new things to learn about an instrument all the time. So you can't afford to put it down".

Irene Chigamba, who plays drums, says that it takes a lot of perseverance. "The first few days breasts can be affected, the palms turn red-hot, but I kept on playing the drums. Even under the arms it was painful, but with the help of physical fitness for instance, jogging and stretching the body every morning helped. With time I got used and it was no longer painful". This might be the reason why other women do not like playing drums. Irene says that women should learn to persevere, and create time, if they are to learn how to play any instrument. It helps to play instruments as women, because it enables them to be in charge of their music.

Tambudzayi Hwaramba encourages young women musicians to explore their creativity through real instruments instead of using computers as this will allow them more radical creativity and freedom.

Tambudzayi would like to see a proliferation of music schools in Zimbabwe, where female musicians will be able to attend music lessons with no strings attached and no fear of being taken advantage of by male counterparts. "At the moment, men get to educate each other in music but women don't get the same opportunities. The creation of more music schools would build a neutral and fair environment in which female musicians could learn and thrive". She said.

It is important for institutions and families to support women musicians.
Stella Chiweshe could not have been the mbira queen today if it was not for her uncle, Gumboreshumba, who was willing to teach her the instrument.

When Stella Chiweshe was growing up she did not understand why women in her area were not encouraged to play mbira. She asked her grandfather and was told that women where supposed to stay at home. She now understands as she herself is always on the road. Women who played mbira when Stella was growing up were supposed to play at biras (night virgils) and men did not like their wives going to these virgils. Some of these biras were held far from their homes. This was not good for the women as they would travel afar, and yet they were supposed to be looking after the home. Women were also discouraged from playing mbira when they got married. They were seen as outsiders who were not related to the family they had married into. So they could not evoke the spirits of that particular family. This meant that it was not easy for women to play mbira before and after they got married. They would be reminded that they were treading in a men's territory.

Lack of encouragement has also contributed to most women not playing musical instruments. Women have been able to play instruments through sheer determination. But some of them have had encouragement from, mostly, their families. In most of these families musical instruments are part of the furniture, and they become part of the woman musician's life.

Chiwoniso Maraire's father, Dumisani Maraire, encouraged his daughter by playing mbira with her. Despite having spent the day working, when Dumisani got home he would play mbira to his daughter. Chiwoniso would ask her father to play mbira for her before she went to sleep. Besides mbira music being a lullaby for her, Chiwoniso learnt a lot from the way her father played the instrument. She was a great imitator. This resulted in Chiwoniso playing mbira at the age of four. She would pick up the instrument in the house until her father gave her, her first mbira. At the age of nine she was already playing on stage with her parents, brothers and sisters. She was allowed to learn, have time to practice until she got it right. "I was just born into an environment where there was teaching in the house. So there was music playing like 24 hours and 7 days, a week, all of the time. If you wanted to walk in the rehearsal room you could. They never fussed about us being in their space where they were teaching and playing. They loved us being there. So it was just a natural thing. It came out naturally."

Penny Yon, a jazz musician who has made it as one of the few women guitarists, owes her success to her family who understood her and encouraged her talent. Her father sacrificed to pay for piano lessons in the 60's. He even enrolled her into a multiracial school and she was one of the few non-whites at the school. This was to make sure that she got good education and be able to have piano lessons. Her mother bought her a second hand acoustic guitar, for $17.00, which at that time it, was a lot of money. She sacrificed so that her daughter could learn how to play the instrument. Penny was not required to cook, which is expected of many girls. Cooking for the family takes a lot of personal time from women. "My father used to listen to my piano. I used to spend at least one hour when I was a small child. I can say when other kids where doing their cooking with their mums in the kitchen preparing supper, I was busy on my piano. I am a very poor cook."

Penny attributes the lack of instruments as a setback to many women musicians. The lack of instruments has hampered women musicians' success. Even for them to play instruments, it becomes difficult, because for one to learn how to play an instrument, they have to have their own instrument that they can use for practice. Women musicians lament not having access to instruments, as it is important for women to have instruments of their own.

One of the biggest resources a female musician can have is access to other musicians, and not just the instruments. It is highly difficult for female musicians to make full use of this resource without risking their reputation or integrity. Tambudzayi Hwaramba says, "In a male dominated industry, it means that they would have to spend quality-sharing time with male musicians. Unfortunately, they are often frowned upon when they do this. What's more? It is difficult to trust that every male musician is only interested in your professional worth and nothing else."

Women who have access to resources such as musical instruments have more time to spend with the instrument, learning from their mistakes and improving. Laura Bezuidenhout who was the only woman in the group Movement of the 1970's, was also lucky to get proper skills through an institution (school), which helped to ground her into the instrument and also help her understand the theatrical aspects of the instrument.

Laura Bezuidenhout played piano when she joined the group. She performed with the group for 7 years. "I grew up with an acoustic piano at home. I would listen to tunes on the radio and then go and fiddle on the piano until I could play these tunes. I had a good ear right from the start. My parents made me take classical piano lessons when I started primary school. It gave me a good theoretical grounding."

Since many women spend most of their time in the kitchen, they should be innovative enough and turn everything in the kitchen into instruments and not to only depend on their voice as an instrument. Women, long time ago, used everything they touched as instruments when they were doing their various chores: pounding, grinding, kupura zviyo (thrashing rapoko), everything.

Women use music – your voice and instruments to celebrate life and womanhood.

Date

Meylene Chenjerayi

A PROFESSIONAL dancer, the third generation of two of the most famous names in the annals of Zimbabwean female artistry, Meylene is the daughter of Jane and the granddaughter of Susan Chenjerayi. She has travelled abroad showcasing her talent, has been to Checkslovakia, Botswana, South Africa, France and Canada where she spent ten months on a Cultural Exchange programme.

Meylene got into dancing while she was still at school. After attending dancing lessons which were instructed by a dancer from the Tumbuka dance company, she was awarded a scholarship to go and dance at the National School of Barley. After training with the National School of Barley she joined the Dance Foundation Course where she spent a year and then joined Tumbuka Dance Company. Meylene's talent has been natured to fruition, by Tumbuka making her one of the top dancers in the country.

Her mother and her grandmother gives her all the support she needs and she says "As a family we inspire one another and we sit and discuss to get the best from each other." Said the energetic Meylene.

In 2006 she was one of the Four Daughter who performed on the Women Musicians of Zimbabwe album, although she was reluctant to lend her music talents to this album seeing herself as a only a dancer, the producer of the project (Joyce Jenje) insisted, knowing there was music in the genes. Here the third generation, despite those self-doubts, acquits herself with aplomb. She did three songs on the album, one by her mother- Usandimirire Pagedhi, another by her grandmother – Mwedzi Muchena and the last one by Faith Dauti –Hama Nevabereki. Despite those self-doubts, she did very well on the album and she cannot believe how her own voice.

Chengetai Razemba

CHENGETAI Razemba is a vocalist and guitarist who has taken Zimbabwean music internationally and blended it with other rhythms to bring out what she calls Rainbow music. Because Zimbabwe is not confined to one style this also encouraged Chengetai to come up with Rainbow music. She is grateful to having grown up in Zimbabwe because it made her who she is today. We called our music "rainbow" because there are different musical styles: jazz, soul, Afrobeat, pop, reggae, rock. She is making waves with this genre in Paris were she is based. Chengetai has just released her third album Zimblue which is half name of Zimbabwe and blue is for the blues. Her orchestra is made up of people she met in Paris including her manager.

Chi Chi as she is affectionately known has been involved in a number of successful projects, she is the founding member of the Zimbabwean group called Afrika Revenge.

She was part of the Women Voices of Zimbabwe (The Four Daughters) and she did her rendition of three songs; 'Ngatipemberei', Mali E Shabeen' and 'Kwamrewa'. Her great voice gave the songs a fresh outlook without taking its originality away, her voice projection, it is captivating and refreshing. Some of musicians who inspire her music are Miriam Makeba, Stella Chiweshe, Oliver Mutukudzi, Chiwoniso Marairie, Lebo Matosa and Shingai Shoniwa.

She would like to pass on the African traditions through music, that were passed to her by her parents and grandparents.

She is working on a new album and it will be about her life in Zimbabwe, South Africa, New York, in Paris and all the countries she has toured.

Maita Jazz Women's Band

EVEN if they have gone quite, the musical group Maita will go down in the history of Zimbabwe as one of the few women musicians who were serious about playing musical instruments. An all-female group, the Maita Jazz Women's band, was a novel outfit which spelt out its own niche in the jazz circles during 2000 -2006. The group was always raring to go, with all members of the band playing instruments.

The group's artists qualified from the Zimbabwe College of Music, in a special programme funded by the Swedish International Development Agency. Ultimately, the group fine-tuned their expertise during their spare time, at their own cost. The saxophonists continued with their studies as individual students at the College.

Dedication and sacrifice ultimately paid off - Maita was a smart group and a force to reckon with during their time. They were masters with experience several years' more than how long they had been in the business.

The band consisted of: Susan Ndawi - drums/rhythm guitar; Shamiso Chitsinde - bass; Stella Mkundu (Mamvura) – lead guitar, Sophia Madzivanyika (J.B) – bass guitar/voice; Anna Matondo Sharai/Saru – rhythm; Marita Tafirenyika (Seby) - keyboard/voice; the youngest, Victoria Zimuwandeyi (Nakai) - saxophone/voice; and Dadirayi Manase (Choks) - saxophone/percussion, who is also the leader of the band.

One of the members of the groups Victoria Zimuwandeyi participated in the CD/album - Women's Voices of Zimbabwe and she did three songs ('Baba Va Boyi', 'Tatetereka' and 'Kundenderedzana'), her voice is captivating. She also holds a Degree in Music from the Zimbabwe College Of Music and this album represents her first work as a vocalist. The group used to perform at different venues and also played at private functions and clubs.

Kundisai Mutero

KUNDISAI Mutero has made her name in Zimbabwean music as an accomplished acapella musician. Her greatest instrument is her voice and acapella provides her the forum to express herself. She is in the process of writing her own songs but for now she takes pleasure in singing copyrights. "I enjoy taking a melody and CHANGING the lyrical content to make it suitable for our performances and I thrive on introducing a satirical flair to the songs so as to rock the audience with laughter so that it adds a little lightness to all our recitals! I particularly LOVE, re-arranging songs and presenting them differently so as to totally surprise the audience." Kundisai is a real pleasure to listen to her acapella renditions. Before starting her group Africa Voice, she was a member of the group Big Sister. Kundisai Mtero's repertoire is influenced by; Gospel, Spirituals, Soul, Blues, Jazz, Afro-jazz, Contemporary, African Traditional and, Reggae. Her upbringing contributed to the way she expresses herself musically.

Although women musicians who have support from their families that has shaped their confidence, they are times when they are reminded by society that they are women in public space. "The reminder is always there especially in our African society…you feel and hear it from your audience from their comments, reactions (i.e. wolf whistles etc) I feel I'm at a greater advantage coz nothing can beat support from your core or nuclear family."

Kundisai also directs and conducts the ST.Georges College Senior and Junior Boys' Choirs which she has been doing for the last three years. "I started when Ava Rogers left St.Georges for the U.K. I enjoy all of this thoroughly as it's such a relaxing and thereuputic change from my Optometry Practice which is my core profession."

Date

Date

Date

Confidence Helps Create Personality
All Female Musical Groups

Being able to survive in public space has to do with a number of factors and confidence plays a major role in contributing to creating personality and the understanding of the complexities of public space. Formal education played a significant role in boosting the confidence of women in post pre-colonial era as it became a requirement one was measured with. In 1954, for instance, Victoria Chingate, who was working at the Harare Hospital as a senior nursing sister having been trained at Baragwanath Hospital, formed the Gay Gaieties. She came to work in Harare after marrying Scotting Chingate whom she met while training as a social worker in Johannesburg. Victoria revolutionized the music industry in Zimbabwe by establishing the first all female group, which consisted of the first female trainees at the Harare Hospital. The Gay Gaeties line-up comprised of: Tetiwe Solani, Grace Mandishona, Dorcas Fry, Martha Mabena, Tabeth Kanyowa, Ruth Jero and Rose Samkange.

An All Female Group was a new phenomenon and in some cases society went to the Gay Gaeities shows out of curiosity to see an all female group. In an interview that I had with Bill Saidi, one of the early township musicians and a long time serving journalist, in 1992, he said the formation of the Gay Gaeties was a real new trend.

Victoria Chingate formed the Gay Gaieties as a way of creating entertainment mainly at Christmas, for the patience and staff at Harare Hospital.
The Gay Gaieties' fan base was composed of a wide spectrum of society and amongst them political leaders who were mostly brought by Victoria Chingate's husband Scotting Chingate who was a politician and MP for Rhodesia and Nyasaland. Having patrons who had clout in society and also who were financially sound added value to their group and this also added to their economic viability.

The group was also fortunate in that there were themselves employed although the rest of the group was still training they were paid a salary and Victoria Chingate was a nursing sister, this was a plus to them and there were able to finance their group adequately. There were able to form an all female group because they were financially sound. During the 1950's not many women were financially sound as they were still new to the urban areas. The Gay Gaeties could buy their own musical costumes; they could pay for backing vocals and were able to pay for the venue. This made music a viable venture and something to be proud of.

The Gay Gaeties destroyed the myth that music was for the so called 'social misfits' who were not (formally) educated but also for the educated. Although at first people were surprised how educated people like Victoria Chingate and the nurses could go for a profession which they thought was for the uneducated. Some were also surprised what an all female group was doing in a public like that, Victoria Chingate was confronted by a female teacher after their performance, the female teacher seemed to have come to the show to confirm her suspicion, "When I came to the show I wanted to see what a woman can do in a public like this, but the music was good and I had fun, and I don't see anything wrong with it."

The teaching profession itself was associated with new values that were to a large extent influenced by Christianity and the so called civilisation.
Despite their mindset that of being moralistic correct, professional women also wanted to have time out and for them to see other women perform on stage as it was refreshing even though unusual. According to Tutu Malamufumu an actor, she says that it is important for women performers to have women in the audience as they become their cheerleaders and also influence performance and gives them courage. She also says this helps to shape lyrics that are influenced by other women unlike performing for men only, one feels a vacuum that ends up influencing lyrics and performance from a male point of view. Therefore it is important for women to be economically empowered across the board as they become independent and it allows them to pay for their entertainment and this way supporting other women.

The Gay Gaeities also produced plays that were educational, one of their famous play was about a woman who was refusing to have her child operated on, and in this play they were trying to allay the woman's fears. This went down very well with the hospital authorities. Their involvement in music and drama raised their status at the hospital as black nurses.

There was also another nursing sister to lead a musical group in the 1950's and she also revolutionarised the music scene by her dance, she twisted and wriggled her waistline compared to the soft dance by other women musicians.
Sylvia Sondo originally from South Africa and was also a nursing sister by profession, came to settle in Harare after marrying Sonny Sondo who was the leader of the City Quads. Sylvia graced the music scene in the 1950's with an all female troupe called The Yellow Blues, they combined township jazz music with dance music mostly Rhumba music. One of the most popular female musicians of the 60's-70's Susan Chenjerayi did her apprenticeship with Sylvia Sondo. Sylvia Sondo's shows became popular because she could dance unlike the other township women jazz musicians who had a 'sophisticated' way of dancing, being careful the way they carried themselves in the public.

The African Daily news under the column: "Women Set The Ball of Jazz Rolling" reported: "There was a moment, brief though it may be, in the history of Jazz-O-African Townships when women led the men. We can fix this period somewhere during 1954 to 1955. There was a memorable occasion when Vic Chingate's Gay Gaieties jointly staged a concert with another female troupe. It all happened at the Runyararo Hall. Young women leapt and wriggled in fantastic dance-styles. The Yellow Blues, although short - lived, owe their existence to the untiring energy of Mrs. Sylvia Sondo." 11 January 1958.

The two nursing sisters enjoyed a certain level amount of financial independence. Financial independence has been another path that women musicians have used to negotiate public space.

The trend of all female groups continued up to this day but they came in different forms. In the 1960's there were female groups but there were mostly backing vocalists in Simanje manje or Rhumba groups, the Intombi ZikaMtwakazi, is one such group to emerge in the 1960's. The late 90's started to witness all female groups such as Maita Women's Ensemble, which came out of the Saturday Workshops at the Zimbabwe College of Music. All the women musicians in this group played instruments. The Amakhosi Women's group is also an all female group and also the members play instruments just like the Maita Women's Ensemble. Dancing female groups also emerged and these were different from the 1960's as there were just women without any man, there were not backing groups, some of the groups are Mambokadzi and Amavitikazi. Another all female group is Amakhosikazi which specialises in acapella.

Organising women only groups demonstrates that women have reached a certain level of independence in the music industry that of not leaning or depending on men.

We continue to celebrate women who have opened doors, which were once closed for women in the music industry and in many fields and professions across the board

Date

Rumbidzai Gladys Chipendo

RUMBIDZAI Chipendo (Standing) – Zimbabwe Music Educators conducting a workshop with members of ZAME and also with Music Educators from the SADC Region.

Rumbidzai is one person who has been educated to understand the different levels that music operates. She taught music at the Seke Teacher's Training College and also taught at the Zimbabwe College of Music. She started off by training as a general teacher. She then took music as the main subject. She chose music as a major because she loved it. She used to sing in church but for her to understand music she had to be educated formally: "So I took up music and then I did my 3 years training. And, when I went up to teach in the schools, I was one of the music people who would help with music curricular activities."

While she had trained in music for three years, she had to train again as a music teacher in order to have confidence in how music is taught. Music is an important subject, just like any other, and should be taken seriously. One should go through all its various levels: "I went to Hillside Teachers College for one year to learn music, so that I could teach it. And there, I think, I became more confident. I went to teach at Seke Teachers College."

To enrich her music education Rumbidzai studied psychology, and was teaching theory of psychology in education. A two-year National Certificate in Music (NCM) programme at Zimbabwe College of Music where she got a certificate also added to her wealth of music education. Rumbidzai Chipendo is the Chairperson of ZAME, (Zimbabwe Association of Music Educators), which also facilitates exchange programs between students in Norway and Zimbabwe.

Education, in all forms, is vital for the development of women in music, because the understanding of music education leads to the understanding of music in its broader sense.

Tambudzayi Hwaramba

TAMBUDZAYI Hwaramba, who made her name in the urban grooves genre in the 90's, was involved in music whilst still very young. Her mother encouraged her to put her education first, so that she could be a well-rounded, well-informed musician with the choice to do or be anything she wanted.

Tambudzayi continued with music in high school: "By the time we were in our second last year of High School, Dumi (Dumisani Nkala) and I were part of an all-girls gospel band, called Milele which included Farirai Mukonoweshuro, Ratidzai Magura and Nyaradzo Ngwerume."

Tambudzayi's mother, who was a great vocalist and tumbrel player in church, greatly influenced her. She also inspired by Cesaria Evora and Miriam Makeba for their wisdom and how they gained people's respect for succeeding in their careers without selling themselves short. Tambudzai also got encouragement from her musician husband, Roy Gomo: "It keeps me grounded on knowing who I am and what my worth is. It also protects me from being discouraged by those that look down on female musicians."

She laments that few women musicians actively seek to play instruments: "There almost seems to be an unspoken belief that instruments are better played by men and that women are not really that good at playing them. I find that really sad and I would like to see that change."

According to Tambudzai, "Women musicians need to be positive role models so that they can empower other women in the communities they serve."

Netsayi Chingwendere

NETSAYI was born in London were she lived until she was seven, when her family moved back to Zimbabwe, just after independence. She grew up listening to all sorts of music on the radio ¬ American R&B, soul and jazz and Nina Simone and Joan Armatrading.

Netsayi Chigwendere has been performing as a singer since she was about ten, most of her family members sing but she is the only one who took up music as a profession. Her music has been described by her mbira teacher as Zimbabwean traditional music that makes sense to a new generation. "I had all these ideas which I thought I could realise as a film maker and as a painter, but because film is such an expensive medium it's really difficult to express things immediately".

She decided that she wanted to try and put all the different forms of music that inspired her together, she got in touch with Chartwell Dutiro, who has his own band called Spirit Talk Mbira. "I wanted him to teach me about drum patterns, because I wanted to focus on rhythm, but he persuaded me I should learn mbira." Netsayi ended up singing backing vocals in Dutiro's band for two years. Later on she had her full band, simply called Netsayi and they played at different venues in the UK. She went on to work with a group called Pangea, doing gigs in the U.S. and Australia.

After spending a decade developing her reputation as a singer –songwriter in the UK, Netsayi has come home. She has performed on some of London's most famous stages including Royal Albert Hall and the Festive Halls. Netsayi has released two critically acclaimed albums, 'Chiumurenga Soul' and 'Monkeys Wedding' (Refreshingly excellent – Mojo Magazine). She has played live sessions on BBC Radio at the legendary Abbey Road Studios and toured nationally and internationally, both as headline artist and supporting artist.

Now she is back in her hometown Harare and has been perfoming at different venues.

Rute Mbangwa

THE sky can only be the limit for Rute Mbangwa, she has been on a steady rise in the music scene in Zimbabwe.

She is one of the top six winners of a competition to compose the theme song for the United Nations World Travel Organisation (UNWTO) General Assembly which takes place at the Victoria Falls in August 2013

Her music and performance are original, unique, and professional. Her performances are also spiced up by her own renditions of old skool, township & pop music.

The 27 year old mature and energetic Jazz performer /songwriter's musical journey started at Chipawo (Children's Performing Arts Workshop) were she graduated from in 1998 and joined in the formation of the young group Another Tribe, before moving on to do backing vocals with popular Township Jazz musician Tanga wekwa Sando, with whom she gained much experience during studio work and live performances around the country. Towards the end of 2003, she worked with the group Africa Revenge with whom she also recorded as backing vocalist. In 2004 she recorded an eight-track album with Jazz Sensation, entitled "If Only My Heart Had a Voice" which she composed, arranged and produced, followed by a second album in 2007 entitled "Rute goes Kumanginde", another rich collection of what she calls 'afro-trad-jazz' originals, which are proving very popular with Harare music-lovers.

She is part of the Pamberi Trust's Female, Literary, Arts & Music Enterprise (FLAME), the gender development programme which has been running since 2006. Penny Yon, project officer for the FLAME project had this to say about Rute, "Rute embodies hope for the future of Zimbabwean women artists; in a time of uncertainty in the industry, she has forged ahead strongly, working hard and employing a highly professional outlook which has earned the respect of other players in the industry, and is already paving the way to acclaim in the country and further.

Her delivery is strong and true, and her professional behaviour a credit to women of Zimbabwe".

She is currently busy in the studio recording her next album. She also now spends most of her time doing charity work through various charity clubs, namely Lions Club and other service organisations in Zimbabwe.

Date

Date

Date

Tia (Portia Njazi

*I*NTRODUCING to you Africa's very own diva in the making, affectionately known as Tia and whose real name is Portia Njazi is a Zimbabwean artist based in South Africa. She burst on to the scene in 2003 with her chart topping single Boy You Got to Know. The single caused a stir and easily dominated the club circuit. It enjoyed heavy rotation on television and radio.

The first album released, titled Spice It Up, which featured renowned Zimbabwean music professionals; the late Fortune Mparutsa, Sipho "Playboy" Mkhuhlani and Reginald "Steppa" Njazi. The album showed off Tia's exceptional song writing ability and mature vocals. Tia did four videos which were aired on Channel O and MTV Base Africa, Africa's leading music video channels. Furthermore she was invited on Channel O for live interviews on Oboma and Ozone. Tia was also awarded the Best Female Urban Grooves Artist award at the Zimbabwe Music Awards Ceremony that year.

Tia has dedicated herself to become a top rated R'n'B/POP artist in Africa. Tia's music is a fusion of the ever popular R&B/Pop which appeals to a wider crossover audience both in and beyond the borders. Tia's music, elegance and style have attracted the corporate world as she received sponsorship from Regency Casino, Telecel and Goldtech previously. In 2011 Tia released her second album entitled Euphoria which she launched locally at Seasons restaurant and was attended by prominent figures and media personal. Singles from the album are receiving generous airplay on air.

Tia is inspired by likes of the late Whitney Houston, Mary J Blige, Jethro Tull, Regina Belle, Anita Baker, Maxwell, Ryan Leslie, Timbaland, Lira and Marshal Munhumumwe. In addition, Tia has a degree in Communication and Media Studies which she completed at Monash University in South Africa. Certainly she is no pushover. Always an achiever Tia is currently working on material for her a 2013 release. The future looks bright for the diva whose mania seems to be just getting started.

Selmor
Mtukudzi

REGARDLESS of coming from a very musical family Selmor Mutukudzi has cut her own niche in the music scene and she has brought her own unique sound. Selmor's music is a mixture of powerful lyrics and a fusion of unique rhythms. She also married into a musical family the Manatsa family and with this background all her life she has been surrounded with music. In order to find herself she has performed with a number of musicians and bands, it was when she was with Pax Afro Band that she met her husband Tendai Manatsa and they formed their own outfit which Selmor has been fronting and leading since 2005.

Although she had been a backing vocalist in a number of bands, she did not find it difficult to assume her new role as a leader, "I didn't have problems really because I was working with people who were passionate about the music and who believed in me as well and were willing to work so it was very easy for me to lead."

Together with Tendai they have produced two albums before the two albums they had each recorded an album. This year Selmor launched an album called Expressions which is doing well in the music circuit.

With her growing family Selmor had to change her timetable but she still finds time for her music. "Before the children I could do anything, we (with Tendai) could go out and play and live there and not worry but now I have kids that I have to think about. If I am setting up appointments, if I am going for shows, like right now we have been travelling to South Africa back and forth because we have started a promotion for my new album so we have to go there and maybe come back after a week. It complicates things a bit but you know, I wouldn't change it for anything else".

Tsungirirai (Tsungi) Zvobgo

TSUNGIRIRAI Zvobgo affectionately known as Tsungi is one of the few women who have ventured into music management "Female managers in this industry are extremely scarce and I believe they always have been. There will always be chauvinists to deal with in any industry and country. However, I find that as long as you consistently bring value to the musicians you work with and show that you have a pair of "balls" in all your negotiations on their behalf - you earn and command respect at the same time as maintaining dignity. Everything has a negative side but dwelling on it too much can hinder progress and change in the mindsets of people."

She is an artistic manager for Victor Kunonga, Chiwoniso Maraire and Alexio Kawara, "Artist management – particularly in the Zimbabwean industrial music landscape - is one of the most powerful mixtures of all the skills and knowledge I have acquired to date and many of the things I love in life. Zimbabwean artists hold a deeply special place in my heart. I believe they create some of the most meaningful, beautifully superior work - rich in its substance and delightful to behold. It is also my belief that art gives a voice to a people. It nourishes the roots of our culture. "

Tsungi's past education and career-path in the corporate world also has a lot to do with how she ended up in this job. Her education was primarily in the arts and professionally, her work continued to circle various artistic disciplines. She entered the realm of management very early on in her corporate career and then pursued post graduate education in management.

She encourages artists to be careful when looking of a manger, "Managers can make or break a musician's career. Choosing the wrong manager can lead to the artist being financially ripped off and their professional image/reputation being compromised."

Ammara
Brown

MMARA Brown is one of the few women musicians who started singing at a very tender age with her father, Andy Brown, who was at that time married to Chiwoniso Maraire. Amara was introduced to the public when she was young, and that helped her to be a confident musician. She was in the top ten of the 2008 Idols Competition that was held in Kenya. A singer, song-writer and dancer, even as a background singer, she felt inspired to continue on the path of the arts. Between the ages of 11-14, Ammara moved to the USA with her mum and took on studying music where she was involved in both the Advanced Alameda Choir and The Martin Luther King Choir.

She was obviously influenced by westernized culture, so when she returned to Africa she continued to create music in the R&B genre. However, working with and for her father, she became more accepting and entertained by many different genres, i.e. Ragga, rock, and afro-jazz. She continued to exercise her talents, eventually on Zimbabwe's national galas as both a band member and solo artist. Ammara won second place in the nationals, hence went on to represent Zimbabwe in the international talent contest Music Crossroads. Regardless of public pressure and much anticipation, Ammara insisted the recording of her debut album, "Be At the Right Time , At The Right Place"

After completing her high-school studies, Ammara moved to Johannesburg, South Africa where she began studying for her Diploma in Music. She also continued pushing for her solo career, recording songs written and composed by herself.

Ammara is certainly creating excitement within hip-hop artist circles.

Her debut album will be a trying experience; she believes anything created for the true love of the arts will eventually prevail.

Date

Date

Date

Family Support Important:
Public space becomes a way of life through family support for Women Musicians

The family has a lot to contribute on how a woman negotiates public space. The confinement of women when they are young follows them throughout their lives into their adulthood life and being in public space may not necessarily change their perception of how they view public space and themselves. Therefore family structures are important in terms of encouraging and supporting women, particularly women in music, because of the nature of their work, which, is in a very public space. Such support gives them the confidence that it is acceptable to go out there and sing and perform. Family support has helped some women musicians to be able to become musicians and to see music as any other normal profession.

Lina Mattaka and Evenly Juba who entered the music scene in the 1930's were initially part of musical family groups and then went on to sing with their husbands. Being in the music scene with the members of their families, particularly their husbands, gave Lina Mattaka and Evelyn Juba dignity on stage which saved their public persona from being scrutinized by the media, society and their patrons.

Most women who sing with their husbands met their husbands in music circles. For this kind of couple music is seen as just any other job or hobby. Couples who meet through family musical groups tend to take music as a way of life and being in public space for the woman is nothing new. For instance, Francisca Muchena (Mai Muchena) met her late husband Mondereki through their families who were involved in mbira playing at biras. They continued singing as a couple and with their children. I attended performances when she was singing with her husband in the 1990's and she would just take over the stage and shine. Her husband was not worried; rather he would support his wife. Watching their show one could see and feel a positive energy around them. In such a situation inhibiting public space is not heavy for the women involved; they can show their musical talents without inhibitions.

They are times when Mai Muchena would be invited to perform on her own without her husband and the husband did not see any problem in this. However, most couples that perform together end up fighting for attention and fame, and in cases were Mai Muchena was invited to perform alone it could have caused problems in their marriage. Fighting for fame and lime light amongst singing couples seem to be an international problem. Ike and Tina Turner the once famous American couple are an example of how a husband might get threatened by his wife's success and fame. Ike ended up physically and sexually abusing Tina Turner until she moved out of the marriage. Mai Muchena attributes this to insecurity and misunderstanding on the man's part and encourages women not to be intimidated and go for their dreams.

Some of the other women who also shared or share the stage with their husbands are Virginia Sillah-Jangano, Shuvai Wutaunashe and Amai Charamba. Although some of these women started on their own and they met their husbands through music.

Virginia Sillah had started music at an early age and was encouraged by her aunt (her father's sister) who raised her after her mother passed away when she was only three. Sillah's aunt was blind but played a cello and a guitar, she also worked as a teacher for the Jairos Jiri Association, an organization for physically challenged people. The Jairos Jiri Association had a musical group called The Sunrise Kwela Kings that was very popular in the 1960's and 1970's. When she was at Mzilikazi Primary School Mr. Jiri noticed Virginia Sillah's talent and asked her aunt if she could sing for the band. Because Sillah was encouraged by her aunt [and a family associate Jairos Jiri] she discovered that she had a talent that was appreciated and also that she did not have stage fright. Virginia drew her strength and inspiration from her aunt who was a strong woman; she had an idol to look up to in her family. From then on she did not look back. When she completed her secondary school Sillah moved to the capital city, Harare, and joined several bands and sang at various venues. When she joined the Harare Mambos she met her husband Green Jangano.

A family outfit in the 1950's produced the youngest musician of that time, Bertha (Mattaka) Msora. She was introduced to music and acting at the early age of five. While Bertha (Mattaka) Msora was young she featured in dramas and films in which her parents took a leading role. She continued with her acting career in her adult life and she wrote a very popular television drama (series) on adoption in the African Zimbabwean context, titled Nyasha.

Family groups continued to have an impact on the music scene in the 1950's as a way of protecting women musicians, parents felt safe when their daughters (women musicians) were in family groups. For example, Faith Dauti, popularly known as the 'shot gun boogie', came from such a group, The Milton Brothers, which was comprised of her brother and two cousins. Moving in music circles Faith married a musician called Timothy Selani, and they had two children.

Another star musician who came from a musical family is the late Chiwoniso Maraire, Chiwoniso started playing mbira at a very early age. Maraire was in public space at an early age because of encouragement from her parents and later in life she got support from friends and the band she was playing with. She was able to negotiate public space because of the confidence that she gained from her childhood and this confidence helped her to approach the band that she later performed with before she went solo. When she started perfoming in different public venues she had support of family and friends, her father would support her by attending her shows.

Similarly, Jane Chenjerayi, who was popular in the 1970's, was introduced to the public by her mother Susan Chenjerayi who was a musician. As a result Jane was not intimidated by public space. She used to tour with her mother. Chenjerayi had access to public space because of her early childhood in which her mother had paved the way and gave her confidence.

An unusual combination of father and daughter came on the music scene in the 1980's in the popular-traditional music gatherings and shows. Although traditionalists in society complained at first, they later accepted this combination as the man; particularly a father has some authority, which society respects. It was as if he was giving his daughter away to the public – which was his social right since it is the same practice as at weddings (the giving away) and is therefore acceptable.

A young woman musician who made her debut on the 8th August 2008, on Women's Day Nomsa Mhlanga accompanied by her father Louis Mhlanga (on guitar) started her musical career when she was only four years old. Her first musical project was with her father Louis Mhlanga, when they worked on a project, which, had to do with abused children for the SABC.

Like wise, Ammara Brown is also one of the few women musicians who started singing at a very tender age with her father Andy Brown who was that time married to Chiwoniso. Ammara was introduced to the public when she was young and that helped her to be a confident musician. She was in the top ten of the 2008 Idols Competition that was held in Kenya.

Confidence is a crucial component that helps women to rise to a higher level, but all too often before they can get anywhere their confidence is shuttered. Many women musicians have had to prove that music is just like any other profession and build their public persona to convince people that being a musician is work like any other, and this is the profession they want to do. That is why the family has a role to play in creating confidence in women and to support women musicians in educating the society by standing by their wives, daughters, sisters who decide to take music as a profession.

Women continue to create your own space in the public and celebrate your talents and professions.

Date

zimbojam.com

Hope Masike

HOPE Masike grew up in a family were people loved music. "Everyone in my family sings quite well but for some reason I stood out. My siblings took other career routes but I chose Art. I studied Applied Art and Design, then Fine Art, and now Ethnomusicology. I want to become a doctor of some African Studies of some sort." She is one fortunate musician who has support from her family, "I have a very special family because they are very supportive and constructive. This might be so because my father was a painter and music has always been respected in my family. I treasure that so much because that support from your family is important."

As young musician Hope would like to encourage other young women by representing them in a positive manner in the music industry. "I have also learnt that society in general judges women more harshly than men. A wrong done by a female musician is much bigger than a wrong done by a man. Society is quick to label women in music-loose. Because of that I have realised I do not just represent Hope, or just the band but I represent every other person out there-young women, Africans...I have learnt that my conduct is a statement and Hope, the brand does not just stand for Hope. So how I am viewed then becomes a big question. I have a duty to teach society that we deserve more respect as female musicians."

Hope has produced 2 albums "HOPE" (2009) and her latest album Mbira, Love and Chocolate (2012).

Cathy Mhlanga

ALL Cathy ever wanted to do is to be a musician and she has fulfilled her dreams by being just that, against all odds. She tried to do a lot of things but music kept calling her back. "Everything that I did I never felt at home because I wanted to do music so I finally gathered my guts and confronted my parents and said I really wanted to do music. Before my father died, the last conversation that I had with him, he said, 'Cathy I know you are going to go places with this kind of music, you are really saying something, it is so deep, it really touches the soul,' and that was very encouraging."

She gets a lot of support from her husband who even bought a guitar for her. When Cathy plays her guitar it is captivating, she practices everyday and sometimes going up to 18 hours. She allocates personal time to her work and she is among very few women who can play musical instruments. At a show she held at her home and invited some solo musicians like her, she gave a splendid performance, her voice projection, her guitar playing skills, it was enthralling and refreshing. One of the songs that she sang which she has dedicated to her late father was very touching and very original. A great song indeed!

Her shows are held at her home, Cathy's home is becoming a popular venue. "Because I am a nursing mother, that was the easiest and the most comfortable place, my children are there, I can attend my children, and I really wanted a lot of people to come and feel comfortable in a home setting, I wanted a lot of women to come as well, nursing mothers as myself because I know the challenges that come with being a nursing mother."

Zanele Manhenga

Zanele is a vibrant young Musician who hails from the city of Kings and Queens, Bulawayo. She couples her powerful voice with great writing skill producing a modern and traditional delight. Still new in the music industry yet has performed with Zimbabwe's greatest, the likes of Dudu Manhenga, Mbare Trio, Bob Nyabinde, Cool Crooners and the highly acclaimed afro jazz outfit Color Blu. Her music can be described as a cross breed of afro urban contemporary melodies.

Music flows in UZanele's blood as she is a sibling to the great Afro jazz Diva, Dudu Manhenga. Her earliest memories of music date back to childhood, at the tender age of ten, when she and Dudu would sing at family gatherings. Under the mentorship of her sister she has toured South Africa and Mozambique as her backing vocalist.

UZanele has undergone grooming workshops by Pamberi Trust's FLAME programme which is aimed at developing women artists. Through her appearances at the Sister's Open Mic Sessions, UZanele has since developed her stage work to applausable standards.

Her music is inspired by South Africans Thandiswa Mazwai and Siphokazi, her sister Dudu and Chiwoniso Maraire.

With such a background and network of rich musical prowess UZanele is set for great heights in her musical career.

Mya Madzudzo

MYA Madzudzo's musical talent manifested itself whilst she was staying with her maternal grandmother, Joyce Jenje-Makwenda. In 2004 Mya was enrolled in a play-centre/pre-school, which had been established at the Zimbabwe College of Music, as she accompanied "gogo (granny) Joyce" to the Saturday Pop Workshops.

By the tender age of four Mya had proved her outstanding artistry in mbira playing and dance. She then adapted the way she played the mbira tunes on to the piano. She can actually play the mbira without looking at the instrument, and can even put it behind her back, and play.

When (Joyce) was invited by the British-Zimbabwe Society (Oxford University, UK) to talk about her works, Mya opened the talk with a mbira tune.

In 2008 Mya entered a contest at the Coventry Shopping Center Mall (UK), which had been organized by the City Council. She won the contest after singing the song by Beyonce – "To the left, to the right".

Again, at the age of four, Mya wrote her first book - "Mya's Story" – recorded from her and transcribed it into a book by Joyce, her grandmother – making her the youngest writer in Zimbabwe then. The book was the pride of her school, and she was also featured in the Coventry Times for her achievement.

Though now based in the UK, Mya still rehearses playing the mbira almost every Saturday. Her love for music, and the arts in general, lives on and the sky is the only limit.

Name: ....

Address: ....

....

Phone...Fax: ....

Name: ....

Address: ....

....

Phone...Fax: ....

Name: ....

Address: ....

....

Phone...Fax: ....

Name: ....

Address: ....

....

Phone...Fax: ....

Name: ....

Address: ....

....

Phone...Fax: ....

Name: ....

Address: ....

....

Phone...Fax: ....

Name: ....

Address: ....

....

Phone...Fax: ....

Name: ....

Address: ....

....

Phone...Fax: ....

Name: ....

Address: ....

....

Phone...Fax: ....

Name: ....

Address: ....

....

Phone...Fax: ....

Name: ....

Address: ....

....

Phone...Fax: ....

Name: ....

Address: ....

....

Phone...Fax: ....

Name: ....

Address: ....

....

Phone...Fax: ....

Name: ....

Address: ....

....

Phone...Fax: ....

Name: ....

Address: ....

....

Phone...Fax: ....

Name: ....

Address: ....

....

Phone...Fax: ....

Name: ....

Address: ....

....

Phone...Fax: ....

Name: ....

Address: ....

....

Phone...Fax: ....

Name: ....

Address: ....

....

Phone...Fax: ....

Name: ....

Address: ....

....

Phone...Fax: ....

Name: ....

Address: ....

....

Phone...Fax: ....

Name: ....

Address: ....

....

Phone...Fax: ....

Name: ....

Address: ....

....

Phone...Fax: ....

Name: ....

Address: ....

....

Phone...Fax: ....

MN

Name: ....

Address: ....

....

Phone...Fax: ....

Name: ....

Address: ....

....

Phone...Fax: ....

Name: ....

Address: ....

....

Phone...Fax: ....

Name: ....

Address: ....

....

Phone...Fax: ....

Name: ....

Address: ....

....

Phone..Fax: ....

Name: ....

Address: ....

....

Phone..Fax: ....

Name: ....

Address: ....

....

Phone..Fax: ....

Name: ....

Address: ....

....

Phone..Fax: ....

Name: ....

Address: ....

....

Phone...Fax: ....

Name: ....

Address: ....

....

Phone...Fax: ....

Name: ....

Address: ....

....

Phone...Fax: ....

Name: ....

Address: ....

....

Phone...Fax: ....

Name: ....

Address: ....

....

Phone..Fax: ....

Name: ....

Address: ....

....

Phone..Fax: ....

Name: ....

Address: ....

....

Phone..Fax: ....

Name: ....

Address: ....

....

Phone..Fax: ....

Name: ....

Address: ....

....

Phone..Fax: ....

Name: ....

Address: ....

....

Phone..Fax: ....

Name: ....

Address: ....

....

Phone..Fax: ....

Name: ....

Address: ....

....

Phone..Fax: ....

Name: ....

Address: ....

....

Phone...Fax: ....

Name: ....

Address: ....

....

Phone...Fax: ....

Name: ....

Address: ....

....

Phone...Fax: ....

Name: ....

Address: ....

....

Phone...Fax: ....

CREDITS

Page	Name of Musician	Photo
1	Chengetayi Razemba	Chengetayi Razemba's Facebook
5	Big Sister	Ava Rodgers
11	Lina Mattaka (1930's)	Joyce Jenje Makwenda
12	Evelyn Juba (1930's)	Margaret Waller
13	Rennie Jones Nyamundanda (1940's)	National Archives
14	Dorothy Masuka (1950's)	Rob Allingam
23	Gay Gaeties (posing)(1954)	Gibson Mandishona
23	Victoria Chingate (1954)	David Kofi
24	Eileen Haddon (1950's)	Margaret Waller
25	Barbara Tredgold (1950's)	David Tredgold
26	Monica Marsden (1950's)	National Archives
30	Ambuya Rena Chitombo (1950's)	Tawona Muchiya
31	Sylvia Sondo (1950's)	National Archives
32	Joyce Ndoro (1950's)	National Archives
33	Ruth Mpisaunga (1950's)	Ruth Mpisaunga
41	Bertha Mattaka-Msora (1950's)	Margaret Waller
42	Mabel Bingwa (1950's)	National Archives
43	Flora "Zonk-Girl" Dick (1950's)	National Archives
44	Tabeth Kapuya (1950's)	National Archives
44	Tabeth Kapuya (sitting)	Simon Kofi
48	Grace James (1950's)	National Archives
49	Faith Dauti (1950's)	National Archives
50	Susan Chenjerayi singing(1950's)	Susan Chenjerayi
50	Susan Chenjerayi on earphones (1950's)	National Archives
51	Sara Mabhokela (1960's)	Louis Mhlanga
59	Virginia Sillah (1960's)	Tessa Colvin
60	Linda Nemarundwe (Maraire) (1960's)	Paul Novitski
61	Beulah Dyoko (1960's)	The Herald
62	Susan Mapfumo (1970's)	The Herald
62	Susan Mapfumo	Speak Out Magazine
71	Jane Chenjerayi (1970's)	Jane Chenjerayi
72	The Two Singing Nuns (1970's)	Sister Helen Maminimini
73	Laura Bezuidenhout (1970's	Solo and Marcie Chiweshe
74	Rhoda Mandaza (1970's)	Sam Mhirizhonga
83	Shuvai Wutawunashe (1970's)	Shuvai Wutawunashe
84	Ava Rodgers (1970's)	Sam Mhirizhonga
85	Biddy Patridge (1970's)	Biddy Patridge
86	Penny Yon (1970's)	Penny Yon
95	Angela Greenland; "Anjii Greenland" (1970's)	Angela Greenland
96	Stella Chiweshe (1970's)	Piranha
97	Francisca Muchena (1970's)	Margaret Waller
98	Elizabeth Ncube (1970's)	Elizabeth Ncube
102	Irene Chigamba (1970's)	Margaret Waller
103	Daisy Chenjerayi (1980's)	Daisy Chenjerayi

CREDITS

Page	Name	Photo
104	Jackie Cahi (1980's)	Jackie Cahi
105	Debbie Metcalf (1980's)	Debbie Metcalf
113	Chiwoniso Maraire (1980's)	The Herald
114	Busi Ncube (1980's)	flickriver.com
115	Irene Gwaze(Promoter (1990's)	Irene Gwaze
116	Taruwona Mushore (1990's)	Taruwona Mushore
125	Tendai Ziyambe (1990's)	Joyce Jenje Makwenda
126	Nyasha Bare (1990's)	Nyasha Bare
127	Nomsa Ncube (1990's)	Amakhosi
128	Prudence Katomene Mbofana (1990's)	Nyasha Mudimbu
136	Benita Tarupiwa (1990's)	Benita Tarupiwa
137	Naome Makwenda (1990's)	Naome Makwenda
138	Patricia Matongo (1990's)	Patricia Matongo
139	Laina Gumboreshumba (1990's)	Joyce Jenje Makwenda
143	Priscilla Sithole (1999/2000's)	Priscilla Sithole
143	Edith WeUtonga (1999/2000's)	staticflickr.com
144	Julia Chigamba (2000's)	Julia Chigamba
145	Olivia Charamba (2000's)	Olivia Charamba
146	Fortunate Matenga (Sister Flame)(2000's)	Fortunate Matenga
150	Patience Musa (2000's)	Patience Musa
151	Duduzule (Dudu) Tracy Manhenga (2000'S)	Simon Kofi
152	Kudzai Sevenzo (2000's)	Kudzai Sevenzo
153	Nomsa Mhlanga (2000's)	Rob Allingam/Women's Voices
161	Meylene Chenjerayi (2000's)	Rob Allingam/Women's Voices
162	Chengetayi Razemba (2000's)	Chengetayi Razemba's facebook
163	Maita Jazz Women's Band (2000's)	Dadirayi Manase
164	Kundisai Mutero (2000's)	Book Café/Penny Yon
172	Rumbidzai Gladys Chipendo (2000's)	Joyce Jenje Makwenda
173	Tambudzayi Hwaramba (2000's)	Tambudzayi Hwaramba
174	Netsayi Chigwendere (2000's)	bbc.preview.somethinelse.com
175	Rute Mbangwa (2000's)	Fidelis Zvomuya
179	Portia Njazi (Tia)(2000's)	Portia Njazi/ Sean Herbert
180	Selmor Mtukudzi (2000's)	zimbeatnews.com
181	Tsungirirai (Tsungi) Zvobgo (2000's)	www.zimbabweonlinepress.com
182	Ammara Brown (2000's)	Themba Hove
190	Hope Masike (2000's)	Zimbojam
191	Cathy Mhlanga (2000 's)	Fidelis Zvomuya
192	Zanele Manhenga(2000's)	Flame/Book Café
193	Mya Madzudzo (2000's)	Tandiwe Jenje

For more information read Women Musicians Book 1930s to 2013 and Zimbabwe Township Music Book by Joyce Jenje Makwenda. You can also read Joyce Jenje Makwenda articles in Newspapers, journals and magazines.

Acknowledgements

Special thanks goes to the Ford Foundation for giving me time and space to dream
and be able to have a voice to express myself telling the story of Women Musicians of Zimbabwe.
Although the project only included the book and thesis, the time and space that I was afforded by
The Ford Foundation made it possible for me to dream and come up with the diary and also the
children's book on music.

The diary is an easy read while you jot down your appointments.

Read on..
I would like to thank all those who made this diary possible.
Most of you are mentioned in the **Women Musicians Book of Zimbabwe**

I would like to thank all those who made this diary a success.
Thank you all!

Publication Credits

Director of Project/Research/Interviews/Writing/Editing (Overall)	Joyce Jenje Makwenda
Assistant Photo Researcher/ Proofreading	Yolanda Birivadi
Editing	Josephine Jenje Mudimbu
Cover Design	Jeff Milanzi
Cover Photo front	National Archives
Cover Photo back	Book Café/Jazz 105/
	Alliance Francaise
Layout	Yolanda Birivadi
Design and Layout	Jeff Milanzi
Printed by	SP Designs

No unauthorized reproduction permitted.

© 2013 Joyce Jenje Makwenda

P. O Box M163,

Mabelreign, Harare, Zimbabwe

YOUR MENSTRUAL CHART

	JAN	FEB	MAR	APR	MAY	JUN	JUL	AUG	SEPT	OCT	NOV	DEC
1												
2												
3												
4												
5												
6												
7												
8												
9												
10												
11												
12												
13												
14												
15												
16												
17												
18												
19												
20												
21												
22												
23												
24												
25												
26												
27												
28												
29												
30												
31												

About the Author (ZWICCT DIARY 1992)

Joyce Makwenda's nickname is "the Bridge". Since 1985, when she began researching Zimbabwe's forgotten township jazz (from the 1930s to the 1960s) she has reunited many former musicians and created awareness of their role in the region's musical development. What began as a hobby soon became a full-time commitment, which she funded herself through dressmaking and selling homemade samoosas. Now her research has won respect. She gives lectures and produces radio programmes about this rich period in musical history.

"People laughed at a housewife trying to be a researcher," she says. "But a woman must go for what she wants and not wait for permission from men. As a mother you must love your children, but you must also love yourself."

Joyce Jenje-Makwenda in her Archive/Library (2013)

Notes

Printed in the United States
By Bookmasters